BOYS' KNITS

BOYS' KNITS

KATYA FRANKEL

Cooperative Press
Cleveland, Ohio

Library of Congress Control Number: 2012943517
ISBN 13: 978-1-937513-11-5
First Edition
Published by Cooperative Press
www.cooperativepress.com

Models: Anthony, Joseph, Luke, Samuel, and Timothy

digital paper by Sassy Designs Inc
Liebe Erika font by LiebeDesigns

Cooperative Press
Senior Editor: Shannon Okey
Assistant Editor: Elizabeth Green Musselman
Technical Editor: Alexandra Virgiel

Visit Cooperative Press at http://www.cooperativepress.com

For Sophie and Timmy

TABLE OF CONTENTS

THE

PATTERNS

ABOUT THIS BOOK

by Shannon Okey, publisher, Cooperative Press

Why a pattern book full of designs just for boys? If you ask any knitter-parent of a male child under the age of can-buy-his-own-clothing, the answer is clear: there aren't as many amazing patterns floating around out there for boys as there are for girls. Even the girls don't exactly have it easy unless they're the ultra-girly type (calculate the cutesy floral rompers-to-practical outerwear ratio in any girl-oriented pattern collection and weep)!

When Katya first suggested this book to me, I immediately jumped on the idea. I may not have (human) children, but I know a pattern gap when I see it. Almost every parent, let alone knitter-parent we've shown this book during the pre-publication stage, has breathed a loud and dramatic sigh of relief when we told them what we were up to… and I think that's a good sign, don't you?

So whether you've got a houseful of boys, a tomboy who hates pinkyfloralgirly stuff or someone else altogether for whom to knit (honestly, I've already been scoping out the possibility of sizing up these patterns for me!), we hope you'll enjoy the book!

THINGS TO KNOW

Patterns & construction

All of the patterns in this book are seamless designs that are worked from the bottom up towards the collar. The sleeves are either joined with the body at the underarms – and then yoke and sleeve caps are finished together – or the sleeve stitches are picked up at the armhole and worked down. There are a number of different yoke constructions included, from raglans and circular yokes to drop shoulders and fitted sleeve caps.

Each pattern comes complete with a schematic that lists the garment's finished measurements. These measurements include added positive ease and differ from the "to fit" measurements given at the beginning of the pattern. To help you choose the correct size, use the size table at right.

Yarn amounts are given in number of skeins as well as total yardage used, in case you decide to substitute yarn. Those amounts were based on the particular yarn that was used for the sample. Yarn amounts may vary if the yarn is substituted for a different brand or type.

Yarn substitution

A lot of thought went into finding the right yarn for each design, so it is important to choose any substitutions carefully. There are a number of things to keep in mind when substituting yarns. Most yarn labels include a suggested gauge and needle size, which can be a good starting point for selecting an alternative. But besides matching yarn weight and gauge, you should also consider the yarn's fiber content, as well as the knitted fabric's hand and drape. Other things to consider are care, washing instructions, and fiber softness. A slinky bamboo yarn will stretch under its own weight and lengthen if substituted for an all-wool yarn, for example, while a wool yarn with some nylon content (think sock yarn) will stand up to more abuse than a purely animal-fiber one.

Swatching

Circular knitting often produces a different gauge than flat knitting does. For garments knit in the round, your swatch should be made in the round, too.

There are two ways to go about swatching in the round. The most obvious one is to cast on a number of stitches that is approximately double the number given in your gauge, join and work in the round as you would for any circular piece. This works great for larger gauge yarns. For finer ones, however, making a circular swatch of 40-odd stitches is a long affair.

Working a flat swatch in the round is a great timesaver. Swatches done this way are worked on double-pointed needles and on the right side of your piece only. Although the edge stitches in this swatch might ruffle, it produces the same result as a knit-in-the-round piece does, and takes very little time to finish. To make a flat

Are you a process knitter instead of a project knitter? To extend your knitting time and enjoyment AND make sure you like the fabric your yarn is making, buy an extra ball and make a quick matching hat as your in-the-round swatch!

swatch "in the round," cast on at least 4 inches' worth of stitches and work the first row. At the end of the row, slip the stitches to the opposite end of your double-pointed needle and bring the yarn loosely across the back, forming a giant float across the wrong side of your swatch. Keep on working from right to left, knitting on the right side (public-facing side) only. You will have one loop of yarn along the back of your swatch for every right side row.

After making a swatch, measure and make a note of your stitch and row gauges. Wash and block your swatch and measure it again. All gauges given in this book reflect what you would get after washing and blocking your swatch, not before. Always check that you get the correct gauge with whichever needles you use.

Both stitch and row gauge can change significantly after a wash. Generally a simple soak and a pat-it-flat to get your stitches relaxed is enough. But if you suspect that your knitted fabric will grow, make a larger swatch and hang it to dry with some pegs attached at the bottom to simulate the garment weight (in proportion). These "drape swatches" are essential for measuring gauge accurately on non-wool yarns in particular.

Sizing

All patterns in this book are designed to fit chest circumferences that range from 23.5 to 32 inches. A corresponding size based on age is assigned to each chest circumference. This was done purely to show each sweater size's equivalent in store-bought clothes – not to mention that it's easier to remember that you are making a size 6 and not a 26.5-inch chest, for example. However, because there is no such thing as an average-sized child, you should always refer to the wearer's actual chest circumference in order to select your size. Alternatively, you can use the finished garment schematic at the end of each pattern to choose your size.

Size chart

Measurements below are shown in inches / centimeters.

Age	4	6	8	10	12	14	14+
A. Chest circumference	23.5 / 59.5	25 / 63.5	26.5 / 67.5	28 / 71	30 / 76	32 / 81.5	34 / 86.5
B. Back-waist length	9.5 / 24	10.5 / 26.5	11.75 / 30	12.75 / 32	14 / 35.5	14.5 / 37	15 / 38
C. Back width	9.5 / 24	10 / 25.5	11 / 28	12 / 30	13 / 33	13.5 / 34	14 / 35.5
D. Armhole depth	5.5 / 14	6 / 15	6.5 / 16.5	7 / 17.5	7.5 / 19	8 / 20	8.5 / 21.5
E. Center back neck-to-cuff	20 / 51	22 / 56	24 / 61	26.5 / 67	28.5 / 72	29.5 / 75	31 / 78
F. Body length to underarm	9 / 23	10 / 25	11 / 28	12 / 30	13 / 33	13.5 / 34	14 / 35.5
G. Sleeve length	10.5 / 27	12 / 30	13.5 / 34	15 / 38	16.5 / 42	17.5 / 44.5	17.5 / 44.5
H. Upper arm	7.25 / 18	7.75 / 19.5	8.25 / 21	8.75 / 22	9.25 / 23.5	9.75 / 24.5	10.25 / 26

A note on adjusting patterns

Adjusting the body length of any of these sweaters in this book is easy: simply work a shorter or longer body length to the underarm. Similarly, sleeve length can be altered by simply changing its length. But because sleeves are wider at the upper arm than they are at the wrist, you will need to recalculate how many plain rounds are worked between each shaping round.

Modifying armholes is slightly more complicated than sleeve or body lengths because they are linked directly to sleeve caps and back width. These are better left alone, unless you understand the dynamics between them. That said, you might have to change armhole length if your row gauge is off. This is especially important if your row gauge is less than that in the pattern, in which case you will not have enough depth in the armhole for it to be worn comfortably.

To add depth to the armhole:

· In raglans and circular yokes: work extra rows/rounds right after you join sleeves and body and before starting any raglan shaping.
· In fitted armholes: work extra rows/rounds after the initial armhole shaping to lengthen the straight part of the armhole.

See page 16 for more information on making adjustments.

Tips and techniques

Any special techniques that are unique to each pattern are listed in the pattern instructions, but here are some tips on finishing touches that you might find helpful.

Joining a new ball of yarn:
· In seamless garments, joining a new ball of yarn should be done at the sides of the sweater and along the underarm on the sleeves.

Working a stretchy bind off:
· Stretchy bind offs on collars are vital on sweaters knit from the bottom up. One way to add the stretch to a collar's bind off is to work the stitches you're casting off twice. Work two stitches as they present themselves. *Slip them back onto left-hand needle and work an ssk or a p2tog, depending on the second stitch on the left-hand needle. Work next stitch as it presents itself. Repeat from * until all stitches have been worked.
· If this creates a little too much ease, you might want to mix the stretchy bind off stitch with a regular bind off stitch by either alternating between the two, or working one stretchy bind off stitch for every two regular bind off stitches or vice versa.

Finishing the last stitch on a circular garment:
· When binding off a circular piece, the first and the last stitch of the bind off round end up being misaligned with one stitch sitting above the other. To neatly finish the last stitch, follow the photos on the next page.

1. Bind off all stitches and before securing the last stitch cut yarn, leaving a 10in long tail.

2. Pull the tail out and thread it through a tapestry needle.

3. Find the first bound off stitch and insert the tapestry needle under both legs of that stitch from front to back.

4. Pull it through.

5. Insert the tapestry needle into the centre of the last bound off stitch, right where the base of the thread is attached and pull the needle out on the wrong side of knitting.

6. Pull slightly to match the tension of the stitch you created to the bind off chain, secure and weave in the end on the wrong side.

Double decreases

Double decreases are used in shaping where stitches need to be reduced rapidly.
- K3tog – a right-slanting double decrease: Insert right-hand needle as if to knit into the next 3 stitches on the left-hand needle and knit them together.
- Sssk – a left-slanting double decrease: Slip the next 3 stitches onto the right-hand needle individually as if to knit, insert the left-hand needle into those 3 stitches from the front to the back and knit them together.

Short rows

Short rows are partial rows that are used to shape knitting without increases or decreases. In effect, by working only part of a row you are building the depth of that part only, In this book short rows are used to shape sleeve caps and necklines. When working a short row, the pattern will indicate to wrap and turn (w&t). This means that you would wrap the next stitch (see below for instructions), which prevents a hole from forming at the turning point, and then turn your knitting. On the return row the wraps are being picked up and worked together with their corresponding stitches to conceal the gap that the short row would otherwise create.

To wrap a knit stitch:
1. Work to where pattern indicates to wrap and turn (w&t). Slip next stitch onto left-hand needle and bring yarn forward.
2. Slip the now-wrapped stitch back onto right-hand needle, turn work, and continue following the pattern.

To wrap a purl stitch:
1. Work to where pattern indicates to wrap and turn. Slip next stitch onto left-hand needle and bring yarn to back.
2. Slip the now-wrapped stitch back onto right-hand needle, turn work, and continue following the pattern.

To pick up a wrap on the right side:
1. Work to wrapped stitch and slip it onto the right-hand needle.
2. With the tip of the left-hand needle, pick up the wrap from the right side of knitting and lift it over the top of its stitch placing the wrap behind it (as it looks from the RS).
3. Work the wrap together with its corresponding stitch.

To pick up a wrap on the wrong side:
1. Work to wrapped stitch.
2. With the tip of the right-hand needle, pick up the wrap from the wrong side of knitting and lift it over the top of its stitch placing the wrap behind it (as it looks from the WS).
3. Work the wrap together with its corresponding stitch.

Crossing stitches

This technique can be used to hide gaps that can form under the arms on the round that joins the sleeves and body. Join the sleeves and body as instructed in the pattern. Work to one stitch before the end of the round where you first joined the pieces together. Cross two stitches around the gap between body and underarm, using either one of the two procedures described below:
- To cross 2 stitches to the right: insert right-hand needle into 2nd stitch from the front and knit without slipping it off the needle, then knit 1st stitch as usual and slip both stitches off the left-hand needle together.
- To cross 2 stitches to the left: insert right-hand needle into 2nd stitch from the back and knit without slipping it off the needle, then knit 1st stitch as usual and slip both stitches off the left-hand needle together.

Three-needle bind off

The three-needle bind off is used to join the shoulders of garments with fitted sleeve caps. Place the stitches to be joined onto separate needles held parallel to each other and with right sides facing. Insert a third needle into the first stitch on both front and back needles and knit them together. *Knit 2 stitches together using one stitch from the front and one stitch from the back needle again; bind off one stitch from the right-hand needle as you would normally when binding off. Repeat from * until all stitches have been worked.

Kitchener stitch

The kitchener stitch, also known as grafting, is used to join live stitches without leaving a visible seam. Place stitches to be joined on parallel needles with wrong sides facing each other and thread a length of yarn onto a tapestry needle.

1. Insert tapestry needle into 1st stitch on front needle as if to purl, pull yarn through. Leave stitch on needle.
2. Insert tapestry needle into 1st stitch on back needle as if to knit, pull yarn through. Leave stitch on needle.
3. Insert tapestry needle into 1st stitch on front needle as if to knit, pull yarn through. Slip this stitch off needle. Insert tapestry needle into next stitch on front needle as if to purl, pull yarn through. Leave stitch on needle.
4. Insert tapestry needle into 1st stitch on back needle as if to purl, pull yarn through. Slip this stitch off needle. Insert tapestry needle into next stitch on back needle as if to knit, pull yarn through. Leave this stitch on needle.

Repeat steps 3 and 4 until no stitches remain on needles.

Weaving in ends

To secure yarn tails on the wrong side of knitting, follow these steps.
1. With the wrong side facing you, thread the yarn tail into tapestry needle.
2. Working away from the place where the yarn is attached to the fabric, pick up approximately 5 or 6 purl bumps on the diagonal.
3. Working in the opposite direction, pick up the same number of purl bumps that are placed directly under the ones you just used.
4. Repeat step 3 once more, cut yarn, leaving about a half-inch of yarn exposed on the wrong side.

Sewing in a zipper

To insert an open-ended (separating) zipper:
1. Lay the cardigan on a flat surface with right sides facing you and the closed zipper underneath, keeping the bottom of the zipper just above cardigan's hem and cardigan's front edge close to the zipper teeth.
2. Carefully pin the zipper to the knitted fabric. Open the zipper. With the right side of the garment still facing you, sew zipper in place close to the zipper teeth. Turn the finished side over and sew in place again along the other edge of the zipper tape, making sure the thread is concealed on the right side.
3. Repeat with the second side.
4. To shorten the zipper, turn any remaining zipper tape under and sew in place to secure edges. Cut excess tape off.
5. If the zipper is to be installed into a standing collar, sew the zipper in as above to half way up the collar. Fold the collar in half and sew in place on the wrong side keeping the zipper teeth out between inside and outside of the collar.

Care instructions

Always read care instructions on the ball band before washing your hand knits. Non-superwash wools should be washed by hand, while most superwash wools, cottons and synthetic fibers can be machine washed on a gentle cycle. If using a spin cycle to get rid of the excess water, place the sweater in a mesh bag to prevent stretching.

To hand wash your item, soak it in tepid water with mild detergent and leave to rest. If there is visible dirt on the sweater, rub it very gently, taking care not to agitate the fibers too much as this can cause felting. Squeeze out excess water, lay the sweater on a dry towel, roll it up, and press out as much water as you can. Place the sweater on a dry towel and ease it into shape while it's still damp. Do not stretch hems or collars.

Adjustments

Whether it's just adding a little length to sleeves and body or tweaking the neckline, children's clothes sometimes need adjusting.

To determine whether you need any modifications, take the measurements listed on the "Size chart" on page 11 and compare those to the finished garment's measurements that you can find on the schematics in each pattern, remembering that the finished chest size should be 2-4" / 5-10cm larger than the wearer's actual chest size.

The key to altering a part of the pattern is in understanding how changing one part can affect the others. This section will help you understand those variables and make your own adjustments.

> Jessica says: My sons have the ability to shoot up a size overnight, it seems, and I'd hate to knit something and have it be too small almost immediately after I finish it!

Growth spurts are pretty difficult to predict because they vary from child to child and vary in their rate. If you're knitting for your own child, though, you have probably noticed some patterns in their growth. You would know, for example, whether he tends to grow taller every six months or just in the summer. Often children's limbs grow first, with the rest of the body catching up later on. So, if he was wearing the same size clothes for a whole year, this might be a sign that you should make the sleeves an inch or so longer or maybe just knit the next size up.

Body length

Because the lower bodies on this book's sweaters are not shaped, altering body length is very simple. Just add or subtract rounds from the body length in the pattern depending on whether you want to lengthen or shorten the garment. (For example, the shaded area on the diagram, above right, can indicate either rounds added in for extra length or rounds removed to shorten the body.)

Keep in mind that pre-washed fabric length can be different from length measured after blocking. Counting rounds instead of measuring the body length with a tape measure will give you a more accurate result.

Sleeve length

In this book's patterns, sleeve shaping is worked either along the underarm of the sleeve or along the the top of the arm as a pattern detail. In both types, shaping rounds are evenly spaced along the sleeve's length. To adjust the sleeve length, distribute any added or subtracted rounds as evenly as possible along the whole sleeve, placing them between the shaping rounds (as shown, below right).

Armholes

To adjust the depth of the armhole, do so after the initial rapid decrease of the stitches after the body and sleeves have been joined.

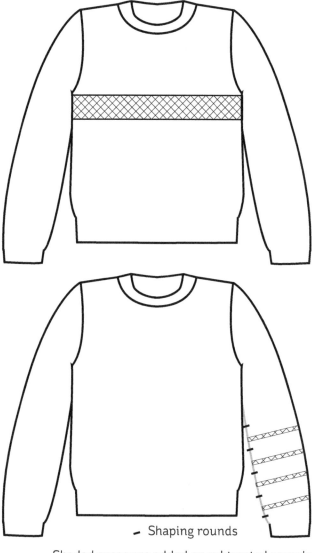

- Shaping rounds

Shaded areas are added or subtracted rounds.

Calculate the number of rounds that you need to add or subtract from the armhole depth and read through the armhole shaping part of the pattern, paying attention to:

a) the type of yoke and
b) how often yoke decrease rounds are worked.

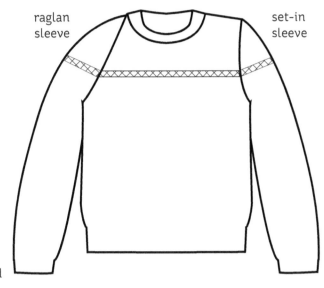

raglan sleeve

set-in sleeve

In a set-in sleeve garment, the front(s) and back are worked even after the armhole is shaped, while the sleeve caps continue to be shaped as you work up to the shoulder. To add or subtract armhole depth in this garment, simply add or skip rounds between the rounds of cap shaping. This will either space cap shaping rounds further apart or bring them closer together and leave your armhole shaping unchanged.

In a raglan sweater, both body and sleeves are shaped simultaneously. Length should be added or removed by working raglan decrease rounds further apart or closer together. Adding length to a raglan armhole can also be done directly after the sleeves and body have been joined and before any shaping commences. But subtracting length should be done in the upper part of the raglan, closer to the neckline. By working decrease rounds closer together, you will decrease the sweater volume more rapidly and if done at the beginning of the armhole this can result in a sweater that's tight across the chest.

Body width

> Stacy says: My son is chubby for his age. I have a hard time finding patterns for him because of this. How do I alter a pattern so that it fits him width-wise without being way too big in the sleeves?

In your chosen pattern, find the size whose armhole depth and sleeve width will fit your child. If the finished chest measurement is too small – if it will have less than 2" / 5cm positive ease around his chest or belly – you can add extra width to the body, while following the armhole and sleeve instructions as written.

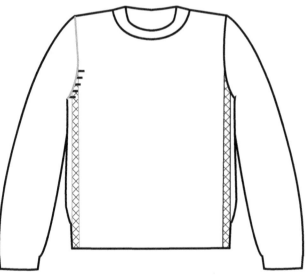

Based on your gauge and your child's measurements, calculate the number of stitches that you have to add to the body circumference. Divide this number evenly between front and back.

Let's say your swatch measures 6 stitches per inch and you would like to make the body 2 inches wider. 6 sts x 2 in = 12 sts have to be added to the body circumference, that is, 6 sts each added to front and back.

After the sleeves and body have been joined, you will need to dispose of these extra stitches so you can work the rest of the sweater according to the instructions.

The easiest way to do this is to consume those stitches in the rounds that are worked even before the armhole shaping begins. However, if the pattern doesn't ask you to work any even rounds before starting the armhole shaping, the extra stitches can be decreased between the armhole shaping rounds. If the raglan shaping is worked every other round, for example, decrease those excess body stitches in the rounds between the decrease rounds. Another option would be to replace k2tog and ssk decreases with k3tog and sssk on the front and back portions of the pattern only, while following the sleeve shaping as described, until all excess stitches have been consumed.

RIGEL

Rigel is a drop-shoulder turtleneck sweater. The body is worked in the round to the armholes, where its body is divided and back and front are finished separately. Both the front and back of the neck are lowered to make sure the collar lays flat. After joining the shoulders, the sleeves are picked up at the armhole and worked down towards the cuff in a wide rib pattern that echoes the verticals of the body pattern. Narrow sleeve caps are shaped with short rows. The only finishing you'll need to do are adding the turtleneck collar and weaving in the ends.

SIZE & SKILL LEVEL

Finished chest circ - 25½ (29, 32¾, 36¼)in / 65 (73.5, 83, 92)cm. To fit sizes 4 (6-8, 10-12, 14). Shown in size 10-12.
Intermediate difficulty – Knit, purl, decreases, picking up stitches, working in the round, short rows.

MATERIALS AND NOTIONS

4 (5, 6, 6) skeins of Blue Sky Alpacas Skinny Dyed Cotton (100% cotton; 65g / 150yds / 137m); #312 Pear.
US4 (3.5mm) double-pointed and circular needles (24in / 60cm long). Adjust needle size as needed to obtain correct gauge.
Stitch markers and tapestry needle.

GAUGE

22 sts and 30 rows = 4in / 10cm in Square stitch.

STITCH PATTERNS

3x2 Ribbing (multiple of 5 sts)
Rnd 1: *P1, k3, p1; rep from * to end.
Rep Rnd 1 for patt.

Square Stitch worked in the round (multiple of 10 sts)
Rnds 1, 3: Purl
Rnds 5, 7, 9, 11, 13: *P1, k8, p1; rep from * to end.
Rnds 2, 4, 6, 8, 10, 12, 14: Knit.
Rep Rnds 1-14 for patt.

(See next page for Square Stitch worked flat chart.)

BODY

With circular needle, CO 140 (160, 180, 200) sts, pm, and join to work in the round. Place a second marker after 70 (80, 90, 100) sts.
Work in 3x2 Rib patt for 1¾in / 4.5cm.
Change to Square Stitch and work even until body measures 9 (10½, 12, 13)in / 23 (26.5, 30.5, 33)cm from cast-on edge ending with an odd numbered rnd.
Next rnd: *BO 4 sts, work to 4 sts before next marker, BO 4 sts; rep from * once more. 62 (72, 82, 92) sts on each half.
Place front sts on holder and cont over back sts only.

UPPER BACK

Rejoin yarn with WS facing and work 1 row even.
Dec row (RS): K1, k2tog, work to last 3 sts, ssk, k1. (2 sts dec'd.)
Rep Dec row on every RS row 0 (2, 2, 2) times more. 60 (66, 76, 86) sts.
Work even until armholes measure 4¾ (5½, 6¼, 7¼)in / 12 (13.5, 15.5, 18.5)cm, ending with a WS row.

Shape right shoulder and neck:
Row 1 (RS): Work 18 (20, 23, 27) sts, turn.
Row 2 (WS): Work even.
Row 3: Work to last 4 sts, k2tog, k2. (1 st dec'd.)
Rep Rows 2-3 once more. 16 (18, 21, 25) sts.
Work 3 rows even. Place sts on holder.

Shape left shoulder and neck:
Place next 24 (26, 30, 32) sts on a holder for back neck.
Join yarn to rem 18 (20, 23, 27) sts with RS facing.
Row 1 (RS): Work even.
Row 2 (WS): Work even.
Row 3: K2, ssk, work to end. (1 st dec'd.)
Rep Rows 2-3 once more. 16 (18, 21, 25) sts.
Work 3 rows even. Place sts on holder.

UPPER FRONT

Join yarn with WS facing and work same as for Upper Back until armholes measure 3½ (4¼, 5, 6)in / 9 (10.5, 12.5, 15)cm, ending with a WS row.

Shape left shoulder and neck:
Row 1 (RS): Work 22 (24, 27, 31) sts, turn leaving rem sts unworked.
Row 2 (WS): Work even.
Row 3: Work in patt to last 4 sts, k2tog, k2. (1 st dec'd.)
Rep Rows 2-3 another 5 times. 16 (18, 21, 25) sts. Work even until armhole measures same as back to shoulder. Join to back using a 3-needle bind off.

Shape right shoulder and neck:
Place next 16 (18, 22, 24) sts on a holder for front neck.
Join yarn to rem 22 (24, 27, 31) sts with RS facing.
Row 1 (RS): Work even.
Row 2 (WS): Work even.
Row 3: K2, ssk, work to end. (1 st dec'd.)
Rep Rows 2-3 another 5 times. 16 (18, 21, 25) sts. Work even until front armhole measures same as back. Join to back using a 3-needle bind off.

SLEEVES

Using dpns, with RS facing, and starting in the middle of underarm bind off, pick up and knit 4 sts, pick up and knit 30 (34, 38, 44) sts along one side of armhole to shoulder seam, pick up and knit 30 (34, 38, 44) sts along the other side of armhole, pick up and knit 4 sts from underarm, pm for beg of rnd. 68 (76, 84, 96) sts.

Set up sleeve stitch patt:
Rnd 1: K4 (3, 2, 3), *p1, k8, p1; rep from * to last 4 (3, 2, 3) sts, knit to end.
Rnd 2: K23 (27, 31, 37), pm, k22, pm, knit to end.

Begin short rows:
Rnd 3: Work in patt as set by Rnd 1 to second marker, sm, w&t.
Rnd 4: Sl1, purl to second marker, sm, w&t.
Rnd 5: Sl1, work in patt to last wrapped st, pick up the wrap and knit it tog with wrapped st, w&t.
Rnd 6: Sl1, purl to last wrapped st, pick up the wrap and purl it together with wrapped st, w&t.
Rep Rnds 5-6 until sleeve cap measures approx 1½in / 4cm from shoulder seam, ending with a WS row. Remove the 2 markers in the center of the sleeve.
Next rnd (RS): Work in patt to underarm marker. Remainder of sleeve is worked in the round.

Next rnd: Work all sts in patt. When you reach the last st you wrapped on the WS, hide the wrap by working an ssk (slip wrap and wrapped st tog as if to knit, insert LH needle into these 2 sts and knit them together). Work 4 (8, 8, 0) rnds even.

Dec rnd: K2tog, work in patt to last 2 sts, ssk. (2 sts dec'd.)
Rep Dec rnd on every 4th (4th, 5th, 5th) rnd 13 (17, 16, 22) times more. 40 (40, 50, 50) sts. Work even until sleeve measures 8¾ (11¼, 13¾, 15½)in / 22 (27.5, 35, 39.5)cm from underarm, or desired length.
Work in 3x2 Rib for 1¾in / 4.5cm. BO in patt.

FINISHING

Collar

With dpns and RS facing, starting with the back neck sts, find beg of next patt repeat and join yarn there. Work in 3x2 Rib across back neck sts from holder, pick up and knit 20 (23, 24, 22) sts along left side of neck, work in 3x2 Rib across front neck sts from holder, pick up and knit 20 (23, 24, 22) sts along right side of neck, work in patt across rem back neck sts. 80 (90, 100, 100) sts.
Cont in 3x2 Rib over all sts until collar measures 6in / 15cm. BO loosely in patt.

Weave in all ends. Block if desired according to the ball band instructions.

Square Stitch worked flat

10	9	8	7	6	5	4	3	2	1	
										14
●									●	13
										12
●									●	11
										10
●									●	9
										8
●									●	7
										6
●									●	5
										4
●	●	●	●	●	●	●	●	●	●	3
										2
●	●	●	●	●	●	●	●	●	●	1

Legend:
● purl
☐ knit

(Multiple of 10 sts.)
Rows 1-4: Purl.
Rows 5, 7, 9, 11, 13 (RS): *P1, k8, p1; rep from * to end.
Rows 6, 8, 10, 12, 14 (WS): Purl.
Rep Rows 1-14 for patt.

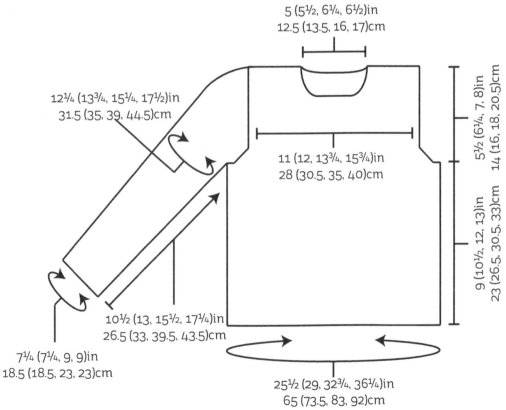

5 (5½, 6¼, 6½)in
12.5 (13.5, 16, 17)cm

12¼ (13¾, 15¼, 17½)in
31.5 (35, 39, 44.5)cm

11 (12, 13¾, 15¾)in
28 (30.5, 35, 40)cm

5½ (6¼, 7, 8)in
14 (16, 18, 20.5)cm

9 (10½, 12, 13)in
23 (26.5, 30.5, 33)cm

10½ (13, 15½, 17¼)in
26.5 (33, 39.5, 43.5)cm

7¼ (7¼, 9, 9)in
18.5 (18.5, 23, 23)cm

25½ (29, 32¾, 36¼)in
65 (73.5, 83, 92)cm

DAX

A charming raglan sweater with large cable panels on the front and back of sleeves. The sleeve increases are cleverly disguised on either side of the sleeve's cable panel. The front neck is lowered down slightly with some short rows while the last raglan decreases are being completed. A simple roll collar gives this sweater a perfectly casual look.

SIZE & SKILL LEVEL

Finished chest circ - 25¾ (27¾, 29½, 31¼, 33, 34¾)in / 65.5 (70.5, 75, 79.5, 84, 88.5)cm. To fit sizes 4 (6, 8, 10, 12, 14). Shown in size 10.
Intermediate difficulty - Knit, purl, cabling, working in the round, short rows, decreases, increases, and picking up sts.

MATERIALS AND NOTIONS

6 (7, 7, 7, 8, 8) balls of KnitPicks Swish Worsted (100% superwash merino wool; 50g / 110yds / 100m); Allspice.
US6 (5mm) and US7 (4.5mm) double-pointed and circular needles (24in / 60cm long). Adjust needle size as needed to obtain correct gauge.
Stitch markers in two colors, stitch holders, cable needle (cn), and tapestry needle.

GAUGE

18 sts and 26 rows = 4in / 10cm square in St st using larger needles.
20-st Cable Panel measures 2¾ in / 7cm wide.

STITCH PATTERNS

2x2 rib (multiple of 4 sts)
Rnd 1: *P2, k2; rep from * to end.
Rep Rnd 1.

Cable Panel (worked over 20 sts)
Rnd 1: Sl 5 to cn and hold to back, k5, k5 from cn, sl 5 to cn and hold to front, k5, k5 from cn.
Rnds 2-10: K20.
Rep Rnds 1-10.

To close cables:
(Right) Sl 5 to cn and hold in back of working needle, [k1 from working needle tog with 1 from cn] 5 times.

(Left) Sl 5 to cn and hold in front of working needle, [k1 from cn tog with 1 from working needle] 5 times.
Note that when closing cables at the top of the sleeves, you may not have a full 20-st panel left because the raglan shaping will have eliminated some sts. To close a cable when the panel is down to 18 sts, for example, for the right cable you would put 4 sts on the cn and hold behind working needle, then work the k2tog maneuver 4 times, k1; for the left cable, k1, then put 4 sts on the cn and hold in front, k2tog 4 times.

BODY

With smaller circular needle, CO 116 (124, 132, 140, 148, 156) sts, pm color A and join to work in the round.
Set-up rnd: P0 (2, 0, 2, 0, 2), [k2, p2] 5 (5, 6, 6, 7, 7) times, k2, pm color B, p1, k12, p1, pm color B, *k2, p2; rep from * to last 0 (2, 0, 2, 0, 2) sts, k0 (2, 0, 2, 0, 2).
Work as est by last rnd for 1¼in / 3cm.
Inc rnd: Knit to B marker, sm, p1, (k1, m1R) 4 times, k4, (m1L, k1) 4 times, p1, sm, knit to end. 124 (132, 140, 148, 156, 164) sts. Change to larger needles.
Next rnd: Knit to B marker, sm, p1, work Cable Panel over 20 sts, p1, sm, knit to end.
Cont as set by last rnd until body measures 9 (10, 11, 12, 13, 13½)in / 23 (25.5, 28, 30.5, 33, 34.5)cm from cast on, ending with an even-numbered rnd of cable patt. Remove A marker and work to first B marker. Do not break yarn.

SLEEVES

With smaller dpns, CO 36 (36, 36, 44, 44, 44) sts, pm color A and join to work in the rnd.
Set-up rnd: P1, [k2, p2] 2 (2, 2, 3, 3, 3) times, k2, pm color B, p1, k12, p1, pm color B, k2, [p2, k2] 2 (2, 2, 3, 3, 3) times, p1.
Work as est by last rnd for 1¼in / 3cm.
Inc rnd: Knit to B marker, sm, p1, [k1, m1R] 4 times, k4, [m1L, k1] 4 times, p1, sm, knit to end. 44 (44, 44, 52, 52, 52) sts.
Change to larger dpns.
Next rnd: Knit to B marker, sm, p1, work Cable Panel over 20 sts, p1, sm, knit to end.

Cont as set by last rnd, and AT THE SAME TIME, inc 2 sts on every 10th (10th, 8th, 10th, 8th, 6th) rnd 4 (6, 8, 6, 8, 10) times as foll: Knit to B marker, m1R, sm, p1, work

Cable Panel, p1, sm, m1L, knit to end. 52 (56, 60, 64, 68, 72) sts.

Work even until sleeve measures 10½ (12, 13, 14, 15½, 17)in / 26.5 (30.5, 32, 35.5, 39.5, 43)cm from cast on, ending with an even-numbered rnd of cable patt. Stop working last rnd 3 (3, 4, 4, 5, 5) sts before the A marker. Place next 6 (6, 8, 8, 10, 10) sts on a holder. 46 (50, 52, 56, 58, 62) sts. Break yarn, leaving a long tail for grafting underarm.

YOKE

Join body and sleeves on circular needle: Beg at the first B marker on center front, work next 41 (43, 44, 46, 47, 49) front sts, place next 6 (6, 8, 8, 10, 10) body sts on a holder, pm color A, work 46 (50, 52, 56, 58, 62) sts of first sleeve, pm color A, knit 52 (56, 58, 62, 64, 68) back sts, place next 6 (6, 8, 8, 10, 10) body sts on a holder, pm color A, work 46 (50, 52, 56, 58, 62) sts of second sleeve, pm color A, work rem 19 (21, 22, 24, 25, 27) front sts. 204 (220, 228, 244, 252, 268) sts.

Work 1 (1, 3, 1, 3, 3) rnds even.
Raglan dec rnd: *Work to 2 sts before A marker, k2tog, sm, ssk; rep from * 3 times more, work to end. (8 sts dec'd.)
Rep Raglan Dec Rnd on every 3rd rnd 2 (2, 4, 5, 5, 7) times, then every 2nd rnd 9 (11, 9, 10, 10, 9) times. Work 1 rnd even. 108 (108, 116, 116, 124, 132) sts rem; 36 (36, 38, 38, 40, 42) sts in front, 22 (22, 24, 24, 26, 28) each sleeve, 28 (28, 30, 30, 32, 34) in back.

Shape front neck:
Note: When you reach the next cable crossing row on the sleeve panels, close the cables as directed above.
Row 1 (RS): P1, work 20 sts of front cable panel, then place these 20 sts on a holder. P1, *work to 2 sts before A marker, k2tog, sm, ssk; rep from * 3 times more, work to last st, w&t.
Row 2 (WS): Work to last st, w&t.
Row 3: *Work to 2 sts before A marker, k2tog, sm, ssk; rep from * 3 times more, work to 1 st before last wrapped st, w&t.
Row 4: Work to 1 st before last wrapped st, w&t.
Rows 5-6: Rep Rows 3-4.
Row 7: Knit to end, picking up and knitting wraps tog with wrapped sts. Do not turn at end of this row.
Rnd 8: Work the sts from center front holder, closing the cables as you go, then knit to end of rnd, picking up and knitting wraps tog with wrapped sts and closing sleeve cables if you have not already done so. Approx 58 (58, 66, 66, 70, 78) sts rem (number will vary slightly depending on when you closed the sleeve cables).

COLLAR

Knit every rnd until collar measures 1in / 2.5cm. BO loosely.

FINISHING

Weave in all ends, graft underarm sts, and block if desired following ball band instructions.

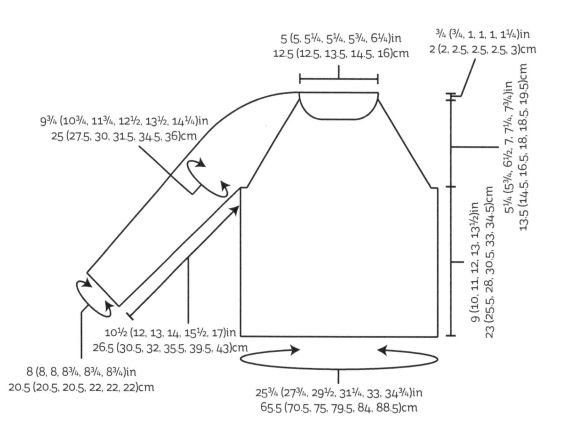

5 (5, 5¼, 5¼, 5¾, 6¼)in
12.5 (12.5, 13.5, 14.5, 16)cm

¾ (¾, 1, 1, 1, 1¼)in
2 (2, 2.5, 2.5, 2.5, 3)cm

9¾ (10¾, 11¾, 12½, 13½, 14¼)in
25 (27.5, 30, 31.5, 34.5, 36)cm

5¼ (5¾, 6½, 7, 7¼, 7¾)in
13.5 (14.5, 16.5, 18, 18.5, 19.5)cm

9 (10, 11, 12, 13, 13½)in
23 (25.5, 28, 30.5, 33, 34.5)cm

10½ (12, 13, 14, 15½, 17)in
26.5 (30.5, 32, 35.5, 39.5, 43)cm

8 (8, 8, 8¾, 8¾, 8¾)in
20.5 (20.5, 20.5, 22, 22, 22)cm

25¾ (27¾, 29½, 31¼, 33, 34¾)in
65.5 (70.5, 75, 79.5, 84, 88.5)cm

EPSILON

This versatile vest is knitted in a single piece from the bottom up. The body is separated at the armhole and the fronts and back are worked individually from there on. The armholes' ribbing and the front bands are knitted on after the vest is finished.

SIZE & SKILL LEVEL

Finished chest circ - 25¾ (28, 30, 32¼, 33¾)in / 65.5 (71, 76, 82, 85.5)cm. To fit sizes 4 (6, 8, 10, 12). Shown in size 6. Intermediate difficulty - Knit, purl, ribbing, decreases, picking up stitches, working in the round, short rows.

MATERIALS AND NOTIONS

3 (3, 3, 4, 4) balls of Rowan PureLife British Sheep Breeds DK (100% wool; 50g / 131yds / 120m); #781 Brown Bluefaced Leicester.
US6 (4mm) double-pointed and circular needles (32in / 80cm long). Adjust needle size as needed to obtain the correct gauge.
5-6 buttons, 5/8in / 15mm diameter.
Stitch markers and tapestry needle.

GAUGE

22 sts and 30 rows = 4in / 10cm in St st.

STITCH PATTERNS

2x2 Rib worked flat (multiple of 4 sts + 2)
Row 1 (RS): *K2, p2; rep from * to last 2 sts, k2.
Row 2: *P2, k2; rep from * to last 2 sts, p2.
Rep Rows 1-2.

2x2 Rib in the round (multiple of 4 sts)
Rnd 1: *K2, p2; rep from * to end.
Rep Rnd 1.

BODY

With circular needle, CO 136 (148, 160, 172, 180) sts. Do not join. Work 2x2 Rib for 1½in / 4cm. Change to St st and work even until piece measures 9 (10, 11, 11½, 12½) in / 23 (25.5, 28, 29, 32)cm from cast-on edge, ending with a RS row.

Separate front and back:
Next row (WS): P27 (30, 33, 36, 38) left front sts, BO 12 sts, p58 (64, 70, 76, 80) back sts, BO 12 sts, p27 (30, 33, 36, 38) right front sts. Place both sets of front sts on holders and cont on back sts only, rejoining yarn with RS facing for next row.

UPPER BACK

Dec row 1 (RS): K1, k3tog, knit to last 4 sts, sssk, k1. (4 sts dec'd.)
Rep Dec row 1 on every RS row 0 (0, 1, 1, 1) times more. 54 (60, 62, 68, 72) sts.
Dec row 2 (RS): K1, k2tog, knit to last 3 sts, ssk, k1. (2 sts dec'd.)
Rep Dec row 2 on every RS row 6 (6, 6, 8, 8) times more. 40 (46, 48, 50, 54) sts.
Work even until armhole measures 5¾ (6¼, 6¾, 7¼, 7¾) in / 14.5 (15.5, 17, 18.5, 19.5)cm, ending with a WS row.

Shape right shoulder and neck:
Row 1: Work 10 (11, 11, 12, 12) sts, w&t.
Row 2: Work to end.
Row 3 : Work 8 (9, 9, 10, 10) sts, w&t.
Row 4: Work to end.
Row 5: Work 6 (7, 7, 8, 8) sts, w&t.
Row 6: Work to end.
Break yarn and leave these 6 (7, 7, 8, 8) sts on a holder for right shoulder.

Shape left shoulder and neck:
Rejoin yarn at armhole edge with WS facing. Work Rows 1-6 as for right shoulder. Break yarn and leave these 6 (7, 7, 8, 8) sts on a holder for left shoulder. Place rem 28 (32, 34, 34, 38) sts on a third holder for neck.

UPPER LEFT FRONT

Join yarn to 27 (30, 33, 36, 38) held sts with RS facing for next row.
Dec row 1 (RS): K1, k3tog, knit to end. (2 sts dec'd.)
Rep Dec row 1 on every RS row 0 (0, 1, 1, 1) time(s) more. 25 (28, 29, 32, 34) sts.
Dec row 2 (RS): K1, k2tog, knit to last 3 sts, ssk, k1. (2 sts dec'd.)
Rep Dec row 2 on every RS row 6 (6, 6, 8, 8) times more. 11 (14, 15, 14, 16) sts.
Dec row 3 (RS): Knit to last 3 sts, ssk, k1. (1 st dec'd.)

Rep Dec row 3 on every 4th row 4 (6, 7, 5, 7) times more. 6 (7, 7, 8, 8) sts.
Work even until armhole measures the same as back to shoulder. Place sts on holder.

UPPER RIGHT FRONT

Join yarn to held sts with RS facing for next row.
Dec row 1 (RS): Knit to last 4 sts, sssk, k1. (2 sts dec'd.)
Rep Dec row 1 on every RS row 0 (0, 1, 1, 1) times more. 25 (28, 29, 32, 34) sts.
Dec row 2 (RS): K1, k2tog, knit to last 3 sts, ssk, k1. (2 sts dec'd.)
Rep Dec row 2 on every RS row 6 (6, 6, 8, 8) times more. 11 (14, 15, 14, 16) sts.
Dec row 3 (RS): K1, k2tog, knit to end. (1 st dec'd.)
Rep Dec row 3 on every 4th row 4 (6, 7, 5, 7) times more. 6 (7, 7, 8, 8) sts.
Work even until armhole measures the same as back to shoulder. Place sts on holder.

FINISHING

Join shoulders using a 3-needle bind off.

Front band:
Using contrasting thread, mark placement of 5-6 buttons, depending on size, on the edge of right front so that the marking is visible on the WS. The topmost button should sit at the base of the V-neck and the bottom button approx ½in / 1cm up from cast-on edge.

With circular needle and RS facing, pick up and knit 3 sts for every 4 rows up right front edge, knit across back neck sts (picking up and knitting wraps together with wrapped sts as you come to them), and pick up and knit 3 sts for every 4 rows down left front edge. Count sts and adjust to a multiple of 4 sts + 2 in the next row if needed.
Work 2 rows in 2x2 Rib.

Next row (WS) make buttonholes: *Work in rib to buttonhole marker, BO 2 sts; rep until all buttonholes are worked, cont in rib to end.
Next row (RS): *Work in rib to buttonhole, CO 2 sts; rep until all buttonholes are worked, cont in rib to end.
Work 4 more rows in rib. BO in patt.

ARMHOLE EDGING

With RS facing and using dpns, starting in the middle of underarm bind off, pick up and knit 6 sts, pick up and knit 3 sts for each 4 rows around the armhole, then pick up and knit remaining 6 sts at the underarm bind off. Adjust sts to a multiple of 4, if needed in the next rnd. Work in 2x2 Rib for 1in / 2.5cm. BO in patt.

Weave in ends. Sew on buttons. Block if desired according to the ball band instructions.

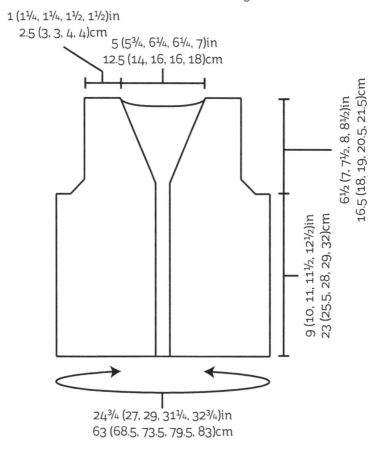

1 (1¼, 1¼, 1½, 1½)in
2.5 (3, 3, 4, 4)cm
5 (5¾, 6¼, 6¼, 7)in
12.5 (14, 16, 16, 18)cm
6½ (7, 7½, 8, 8½)in
16.5 (18, 19, 20.5, 21.5)cm
9 (10, 11, 11½, 12½)in
23 (25.5, 28, 29, 32)cm
24¾ (27, 29, 31¼, 32¾)in
63 (68.5, 73.5, 79.5, 83)cm

FRACTAL

This chunky-weight raglan has a random geometrical pattern on the front that's been set into a stockinette ground. I designed the pattern "free hand" following a simple rule of no more than 4 purl squares (5sts x 4 rows each) for each horizontal or vertical line. The chart has been scaled up and down to be proportional in all the sizes. However, in the spirit of random play, feel free to work up your own variation of stacked checks on your sweater.

SIZE & SKILL LEVEL

Finished chest circ - 25¼ (27½, 29¾, 32, 34¼)in / 64 (70, 75.5, 81.5, 87)cm. To fit sizes 4 (6-8, 10, 12, 14). Shown in size 10.
Intermediate difficulty - Knit, purl, decreases, picking up stitches, working in the round, short rows.

MATERIALS AND NOTIONS

1 (1, 1, 2, 2) skeins of Cascade Ecological Wool (100% undyed Peruvian highland Wool; 250g / 478yds / 437m); #8018 light gray.
US10½ (6.5mm) and US10 (6mm) double-pointed and circular needles (24in / 60cm long). Adjust needle size as needed to obtain the correct gauge.
Stitch markers in 3 colors, stitch holders, and tapestry needle.

GAUGE

14 sts and 20 rows = 4in / 10cm in St st using larger needles.

STITCH PATTERNS

2x2 Rib (multiple of 4 sts)
Rnd 1: *P1, k2, p1; rep from * to end.
Rep Rnd 1 for patt.

(See next page for Chart.)

BODY

With smaller circular needle, CO 88 (96, 104, 112, 120) sts, pm and join to work in the round. Work 2x2 Rib for 1½ in / 4cm. Change to larger needle.
Next rnd: K19 (19, 19, 23, 27), pm, k24 (28, 32, 32, 32), pm, knit to end. Working Chart within markers just placed

and the rest of the body in St st, work even until body measures 9 (11, 12, 13, 13½)in / 23 (28, 30.5, 33, 34.5)cm from cast-on edge. Cut yarn and leave body on circular needle.

SLEEVES

With smaller dpns, CO 28 (28, 32, 32, 32) sts, pm and join to work in the round. Work in 2x2 Rib for 1½ in / 4cm. Change to larger needles and St st. Inc 1 st at beg and end of next rnd, then every foll 8th rnd 2 (5, 6, 8, 9) times more. 34 (40, 46, 50, 52) sts.
Work even until sleeve measures 10½ (12, 14, 15½, 17)in / 26.5 (30.5, 35.5, 39.5, 43)cm from cast-on edge, ending last rnd 2 (2, 2, 4, 4) sts before the marker. Place next 4 (4, 4, 8, 8) sts on a holder. 30 (36, 42, 42, 44) sts.

YOKE

Join body and sleeves:
Starting with front, slip first 22 (24, 26, 28, 30) sts onto RH needle without knitting them; you are now at center front. Join yarn, work next 20 (22, 24, 24, 26) front sts, place next 4 (4, 4, 8, 8) sts on holder, pm color A, k15 (18, 21, 21, 22) sts from first sleeve, pm color B, k15 (18, 21, 21, 22) sleeve sts, pm color A, k40 (44, 48, 48, 52) back sts, pm color A, place next 4 (4, 4, 8, 8) sts on holder, k15 (18, 21, 21, 22) sts from second sleeve, pm color B, k15 (18, 21, 21, 22) sleeve sts, pm color A, k20 (22, 24, 24, 26) rem front sts, pm color C for beg of rnd. 140 (160, 180, 180, 192) sts.

Shape raglan:
Work 2 (3, 6, 9, 10) rnds even.
Dec rnd 1: *Work to 2 sts before A marker, k2tog, sm, ssk; rep from * 3 times more, work to end of rnd. (8 sts dec'd.)
Rep Dec rnd 1 on every other rnd twice more. 34 (38, 42, 42, 46) sts each in front and back, 24 (30, 36, 36, 38) sts each sleeve.
Begin working back and forth: turn work at C marker and work 1 WS row even.

Shape V-neck, raglan and sleeves; PLEASE READ AHEAD.
Work Dec row 2 on every RS row 5 (2, 0, 0, 0) times. 7 (15, 21, 21, 23) sts in each half of front, 24 (34, 42, 42, 46) sts in back, 14 (26, 36, 36, 38) sts each sleeve.

Work Dec row 3 alternating with Dec row 2 on RS rows 1 (3, 4, 4, 5) times. 3 (3, 5, 5, 3) sts in each half of front, 20 (22, 26, 26, 26) sts in back, 8 (8, 12, 12, 8) sts each sleeve.
Work Dec row 3 on every RS row 0 (0, 1, 1, 0) times. 3 sts in each half of front, 20 (22, 24, 24, 26) sts in back, 8 sts each sleeve.
Work Dec row 4 on every RS row twice. 1 st each half of front, 16 (18, 20, 20, 22) sts in back, 4 sts each sleeve.

Dec row 2 (RS): Sl1, ssk, *work to 2 sts before A marker, k2tog, sm, ssk; rep from * 3 times more, work to last 3 sts, k2tog, k1. (10 sts dec'd.)
Dec row 3 (RS): Sl1, ssk, *work to 2 sts before A marker, k2tog, sm, ssk, k to 2 sts before B marker, ssk, sm, k2tog,

knit to 2 sts before A marker, k2tog, sm, ssk; rep from * once more, work to last 3 sts, k2tog, k1. (14 sts dec'd.)
Dec row 4 (RS): Sl1, *work to 2 sts before A marker, k2tog, sm, ssk; rep from * 3 times more, work to end. (8 sts dec'd.)

BO all sts purlwise on the next WS row.

FINISHING
Graft underarms. Weave in ends and block according to ball band instructions.

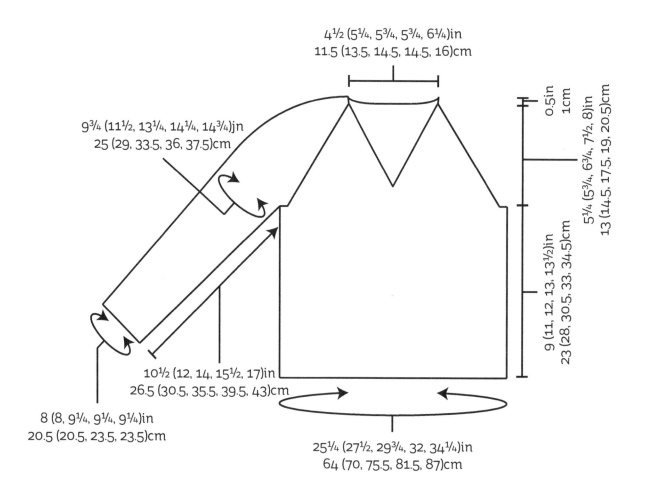

4½ (5¼, 5¾, 5¾, 6¼)in
11.5 (13.5, 14.5, 14.5, 16)cm

9¾ (11½, 13¼, 14¼, 14¾)in
25 (29, 33.5, 36, 37.5)cm

0.5in
1cm

5¼ (5¾, 6¾, 7½, 8)in
13 (14.5, 17.5, 19, 20.5)cm

9 (11, 12, 13, 13½)in
23 (28, 30.5, 33, 34.5)cm

10½ (12, 14, 15½, 17)in
26.5 (30.5, 35.5, 39.5, 43)cm

8 (8, 9¼, 9¼, 9¼)in
20.5 (20.5, 23.5, 23.5)cm

25¼ (27½, 29¾, 32, 34¼)in
64 (70, 75.5, 81.5, 87)cm

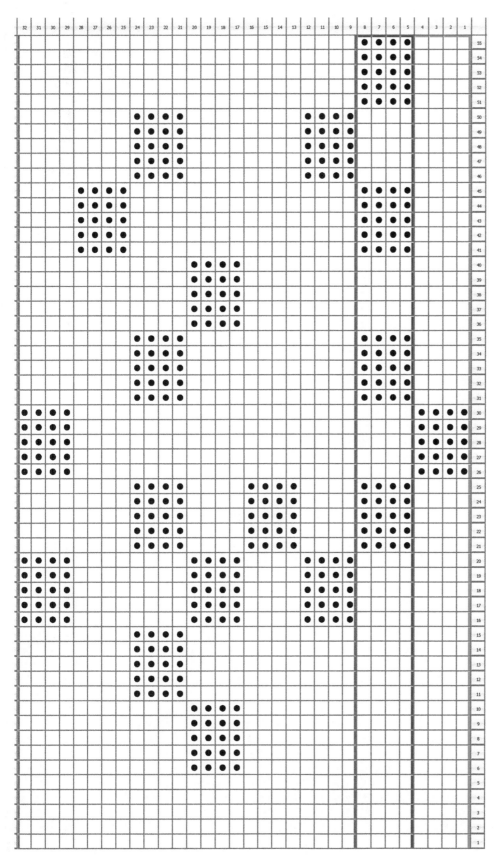

Legend:

☐ knit

● purl

Chart notes

For size 25¼in, work chart stitches 9-32; for size 27½in, work chart stitches 5-32; for all other sizes, work chart stitches 1-32.

LANDON

Off-center purl ridges on the front of the body and the opposite sleeve add just enough interest to the knitting, while still keeping the pullover simple enough to wear.

SIZE & SKILL LEVEL

Finished chest circ - 25½ (27, 28½, 30, 32, 34)in / 65 (68.5, 72.5, 76, 81.5, 86.5)cm. To fit sizes 4 (6, 8, 10, 12, 14). Shown in size 6.

Intermediate difficulty - Knit, purl, decreases, picking up stitches, working in the round, short rows.

MATERIALS AND NOTIONS

6 (6, 6, 7, 7, 8) balls of Garnstudio DROPS Alaska (100% wool; 50 g/ 82 yds / 75m); #52 dark turquoise.
US6 (4mm) and US7 (4.5mm) double-pointed and circular needles (24in / 60cm long). Adjust needle size as needed to obtain correct gauge.
Stitch markers and tapestry needle.

GAUGE

16 sts and 21 rows = 4in / 10cm square in St st using larger needles.

STITCH PATTERNS

3x3 Rib (multiple of 6 sts)
Rnd 1: *K3, p3; rep from * to end.
Rep Rnd 1 for patt.

2x2 Rib (multiple of 4 sts)
Rnd 1: *K2, p2; rep from * to end.
Rep Rnd 1 for patt.

Ridge pattern worked in the round
Rnds 1-2: Knit.
Rnds 3-4: Purl.
Rep Rnds 1-4 for patt.

Ridge pattern worked flat
Row 1 (RS): Knit.
Rows 2-3: Purl.
Row 4: Knit.
Rep Rows 1-4 for patt.

BODY

With smaller circular needle, CO 102 (108, 114, 120, 126, 138) sts, pm and join to work in the round. Work in 3x3 Rib for 1½in / 4cm.
Change to larger needle. Knit 1 rnd, inc 0 (0, 0, 0, 2, 0) / dec 0 (0, 0, 0, 0, 2) sts evenly spaced. 102 (108, 114, 120, 128, 136) sts.
Set up ridge patt: K28 (30, 32, 34, 36, 40), pm, work 14 (15, 16, 17, 18, 19) sts in Ridge patt, pm, knit to end. Working sts within markers in Ridge patt and the rest of the body in St st, work even until body measures 9 (10, 11, 12, 13, 13½)in / 23 (25.5, 28, 30.5, 33, 34.5)cm from cast-on edge.
Next rnd: *BO 3 sts, work in patt until you have 45 (48, 51, 54, 57, 63) sts on right hand needle, BO 3 sts; rep from * once more. 45 (48, 51, 54, 58, 62) sts rem on both front and back pieces.

LEFT SLEEVE

With smaller dpns, CO 28 (28, 32, 32, 32, 36) sts, pm and join to work in the round. Work in 2x2 Rib until piece measures 1½in / 4cm.
Change to larger needles. Set up Ridge patt: K9 (9, 11, 11, 11, 13), pm, work 8 sts in Ridge patt, pm, k11 (11, 13, 13, 13, 15). Work sts within markers in ridge patt and the rest of the sleeve in st st. Inc 1 st at the beg and end of next rnd, then every foll 7 (7, 9, 9, 8, 8)th rnd 6 (7, 6, 7, 9, 9) times more. 42 (44, 46, 48, 52, 56) sts.
Work even until sleeve measures 10½ (12, 13½, 14¼, 15½, 17½)in / 26.5 (30.5, 34.5, 36, 39.5, 44.5)cm from cast-on edge.
Next rnd: BO 3 sts, knit to last 3 sts, BO 3 sts. 36 (38, 40, 42, 46, 50) sts.

RIGHT SLEEVE

Work as for Left sleeve, omitting the Ridge patt.

YOKE

Place all sts on the larger circular needle in the following order: Left sleeve, pm, Front, pm, Right sleeve, pm, Back, pm. You will have 45 (48, 51, 54, 58, 62) sts in each body section and 36 (38, 40, 42, 46, 50) sts in each sleeve section.
Work 1 rnd over all sts, working Ridge patt sections as set throughout.

Shape armholes:
Dec rnd: *Ssk, work to 2 sts before next armhole marker, k2tog, sm; rep from * 3 times more. (8 sts dec'd.) Rep last rnd 2 times more. 39 (42, 45, 48, 52, 56) sts each in front and back; 30 (32, 34, 36, 40, 44) sts in each sleeve.

Shape sleeve caps:
Work 1 (2, 2, 2, 2, 2) rnds even.
Dec rnd 2: *Ssk, work to 2 sts before next armhole marker, k2tog, sm, work to next armhole marker, sm; rep from * once more. (4 sts dec'd.)
Rep Dec rnd 2 on every 2nd rnd 3 (2, 4, 5, 6, 5) times, then every rnd 6 (6, 4, 4, 4, 7) times. 12 (14, 16, 16, 18, 18) sts rem in each sleeve.

Back sleeve cap shaping:
Working back and forth on Back only, sm, k1 and turn work.
Row 1 (WS): Sl1, sm, purl to marker, sm, p2tog, turn.
Row 2 (RS): Sl1, sm, knit to marker, sm, k2tog, turn.
Rep last 2 rows 4 (5, 6, 6, 7, 7) times more. Place these 41 (44, 47, 50, 54, 58) sts on holder.

Front sleeve cap and neck shaping:
With RS facing and starting at the left front armhole marker, join yarn and k14 (15, 16, 17, 18, 19), BO center 11 (12, 13, 14, 16, 18) sts, k14 (15, 16, 17, 18, 19), sm, k1, turn.
Right shoulder:
Row 1 (WS): Sl1, sm, work in patt to end.

Row 2 (RS): Sl1, k2tog, work in patt to marker, sm, k2tog, turn.
Rows 3-8: Rep Rows 1-2.
Row 9: Sl1, sm, work in patt to end.
Row 10: Sl1, work in patt to marker, sm, k2tog, turn.
Rep Rows 9-10 0 (1, 2, 2, 3, 3) times more. Place rem 11 (12, 13, 14, 15, 16) sts on holder.

Left shoulder:
Join yarn at neck edge with WS facing.
Row 1 (WS): Sl1, purl to marker, sm, p2tog, turn.
Row 2 (RS): Sl1, sm, knit to last 3 sts, ssk, k1.
Rows 3-8: Rep Rows 1-2.
Row 9: Sl1, sm, purl to marker, sm, p2tog, turn.
Row 10: Sl1, sm, knit to end.
Rep Rows 9-10 0 (1, 2, 2, 3, 3) times more. Place rem 11 (12, 13, 14, 15, 16) sts on holder.

FINISHING
With right sides facing work a 3-needle bind off over 11 (12, 13, 14, 15, 16) sts of right shoulder, BO 19 (20, 21, 22, 24, 26) center back neck sts, then work a 3 needle BO over 11 (12, 13, 14, 15, 16) sts of left shoulder.

Collar:
With larger dpns and RS facing, beg at left shoulder seam pick up and knit 1 st in every st and row around neckline. Knit 1 rnd and BO loosely.

Seam underarms. Weave in all ends. Block if desired according to the ball band instructions.

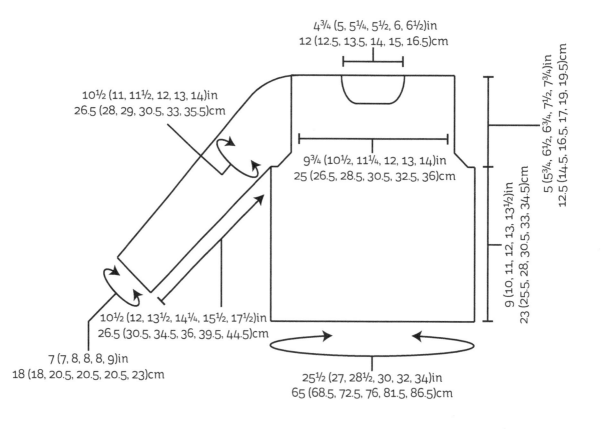

4¾ (5, 5¼, 5½, 6, 6½)in
12 (12.5, 13.5, 14, 15, 16.5)cm

10½ (11, 11½, 12, 13, 14)in
26.5 (28, 29, 30.5, 33, 35.5)cm

9¾ (10½, 11¼, 12, 13, 14)in
25 (26.5, 28.5, 30.5, 32.5, 36)cm

5 (5¾, 6½, 6¾, 7½, 7¾)in
12.5 (14.5, 16.5, 17, 19, 19.5)cm

9 (10, 11, 12, 13, 13½)in
23 (25.5, 28, 30.5, 33, 34.5)cm

10½ (12, 13½, 14¼, 15½, 17½)in
26.5 (30.5, 34.5, 36, 39.5, 44.5)cm

7 (7, 8, 8, 8, 9)in
18 (18, 20.5, 20.5, 20.5, 23)cm

25½ (27, 28½, 30, 32, 34)in
65 (68.5, 72.5, 76, 81.5, 86.5)cm

RYKER

The armholes and neckline on this vest are finished with a knit-in narrow rib that prevents the body from rolling in and completes the vest without taking attention from the textured body. A buttonless Henley neckline can be either dressed up or down.

SIZE & SKILL LEVEL

Finished chest circ - 25½ (27, 28¼, 30½, 32¼, 35)in / 65 (68.5, 72, 77.5, 82, 89) cm. To fit sizes 4 (6, 8, 10, 12, 14). Shown in size 10.
Intermediate difficulty - Knit, purl, working the round, decreases and picking up sts.

MATERIALS AND NOTIONS

3 (3, 3, 3, 4, 4) balls of KnitPicks Simply Cotton Worsted (100% organic cotton; 100g / 164yds / 150m); #C854 Camel Heather.
US7 (4.5mm) double-pointed and circular needles (24in / 60cm long). Adjust needle size as needed to obtain correct gauge.
Stitch markers, stitch holders and tapestry needle.

GAUGE

18 sts and 24 rows = 4in / 10cm in patt.

STITCH PATTERN

2x1 Rib (multiple of 3 sts)
Rnd 1: *P2, k1; rep from * to end.
Rep Rnd 1 for patt.

BODY

CO 114 (120, 126, 138, 144, 156) sts, pm and join to work in the round. Work 2x1 Rib for 1½in / 4cm.
Pattern set-up rnd: M1, k4, p1, *k5, p1; rep from * around. 115 (121, 127, 137, 145, 157) sts.
Work all subsequent rnds as: (K5, p1) around, leaving beg-of-rnd marker in place but ignoring it as you carry out the stitch patt; pattern will naturally spiral around body.

Work even until body measures 9 (10, 11, 12, 13, 13½)in / 23 (25.5, 28, 30.5, 33, 34.5)cm from cast-on edge, ending last rnd at the marker.

Divide for armholes:
Work 57 (61, 63, 69, 73, 79) sts in patt, turn. Place rem 58 (60, 64, 70, 72, 78) sts on a holder.
As you work upper body, take care to keep continuity of stitch patt.

UPPER BACK

Next row (WS): Sl1, p1, k2, work in patt to last 4 sts, k2, p2.
Dec row 1 (RS): Sl1, k1, p2, k3tog, work in patt to last 7 sts, sssk, p2, k2. (4 sts dec'd.)
Rep last 2 rows once more. 49 (53, 55, 61, 65, 71) sts.
Next row (WS): Sl1, p1, k2, work to last 4 sts, k2, p2.
Dec row 2: Sl1, k1, p2, k2tog, work to last 6 sts, ssk, p2, k2. (2 sts dec'd.)
Rep last 2 rows 2 (2, 1, 2, 2, 3) more times. 43 (47, 51, 55, 59, 63) sts.
Next row (WS): Sl1, p1, k2, work to last 4 sts, k2, p2.
Next row (RS): Sl1, k1, p2, work to last 4 sts, p2, k2.
Rep last 2 rows until armholes measure 5½ (6, 6½, 7, 7½, 8)in / 14 (15, 16.5, 18, 19, 20.5)cm. Place sts on holder.

UPPER FRONT

Join yarn with WS facing for first row. Work as for back until armholes measure 2in / 5cm. 44 (46, 52, 56, 58, 62) sts.

Left side:
Row 1 (RS): Sl1, k1, p2, work 16 (17, 20, 22, 23, 25) sts in patt, pm, p2, k2. Turn, leaving rem sts unworked. 24 (25, 28, 30, 31, 33) sts.
Row 2 (WS): Sl1, p1, k2, work to last 4 sts, k2, p2.
Row 3 (RS): Sl1, k1, p2, work to last 4 sts, p2, k2.
Rep last 2 rows until armhole measures 3½ (4, 4½, 5, 4½, 5)in / 9 (10, 11.5, 12.5, 11.5, 12.5)cm, ending with a WS row.
Next row (RS): Sl1, work to last 8 sts, place last 8 sts on a holder, turn. 16 (17, 20, 22, 23, 25) sts.
Next row: Sl1, p1, work to last 4 sts, k2, p2.
Dec row (RS): Sl1, k1, p2, work to last 3 sts, ssk, k1. (1 st dec'd.)
Rep the last 2 rows 4 (4, 5, 5, 6, 7) times more. 11 (12, 14, 16, 16, 17) sts. Work even if necessary, maintaining armhole edging, until armhole measures same as back to shoulder. Place sts on holder.

Right side:
With RS facing and starting at center front, fold the left front slightly towards you, from the edge count back 4 purl bumps behind the 4 edge sts of the left front and join yarn. Pick up and knit 4 sts behind the placket of the left front, one in each purl bump, keeping yarn tight. Work in patt across right front sts to last 4, p2, k2. 24 (25, 28, 30, 31, 33) sts.
Row 1 (WS): Sl1, p1, k2, work to last 4 sts, k2, p2.
Row 2 (RS): Sl1, k1, p2, work to last 4 sts, p2, k2.
Rep last 2 rows until armhole measures 3½ (4, 4½, 5, 4½, 5)in / 9 (10, 11.5, 12.5, 11.5, 12.5)cm, ending with a WS row.

Next row (RS): Work 8 sts as set and place them on holder, work to last 4 sts, p2, k2. 16 (17, 20, 22, 23, 25) sts.
Next row (WS): Sl1, p1, k2, work in patt to last 2 sts, p2.
Dec row: Sl1, k2tog, work to last 4 sts, k2, p2.
Rep the last 2 rows 4 (4, 5, 5, 6, 7) times more. 11 (12, 14, 16, 16, 17) sts. Work even if necessary, maintaining armhole edging, until armhole measures same as back to shoulder. Place sts on holder.

FINISHING

Join shoulders using a 3-needle bind off, leaving 21 (21, 23, 23, 27, 29) back neck sts on holder.

Collar:
With RS facing and starting at the right front, [sl1, k1, p2, k4] over 8 sts from holder, pick up and knit 1 st into each slip-stitch loop along right neck edge, knit across back neck sts, pick up and knit 1 st into each slip-stitch loop along left neck edge, [k4, p2, k2] from the holder. Count sts and adjust to a multiple of 4 sts + 2 on next row if needed.
Row 1 (WS): Sl1, p1, *k2, p2; rep from * to end.
Row 2 (RS): Sl1, k1, *p2, k2; rep from * to end.
Rep last 2 rows until collar measures 1in / 2.5cm. BO loosely in patt.

Weave in all ends and block if desired according to ball band instructions.

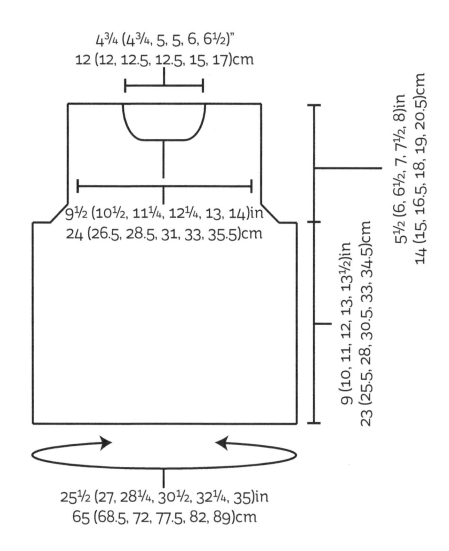

4¾ (4¾, 5, 5, 6, 6½)"
12 (12, 12.5, 12.5, 15, 17)cm

9½ (10½, 11¼, 12¼, 13, 14)in
24 (26.5, 28.5, 31, 33, 35.5)cm

5½ (6, 6½, 7, 7½, 8)in
14 (15, 16.5, 18, 19, 20.5)cm

9 (10, 11, 12, 13, 13½)in
23 (25.5, 28, 30.5, 33, 34.5)cm

25½ (27, 28¼, 30½, 32¼, 35)in
65 (68.5, 72, 77.5, 82, 89)cm

BALEY

Single-ply Malabrigo Worsted is probably the softest wool yarn I have worked with. The lack of twist creates a smooth, slightly fuzzy surface. It's perfect for this simple, textured rib pattern. Hem, cuffs, and collar are all worked in an easy 2x1 ribbing that flows organically in and out of the main pattern.

SIZE & SKILL LEVEL

Finished chest circ - 26¼ (28¼, 30½, 32¾, 35)in / 66.5 (72, 77.5, 83, 89)cm. To fit sizes 4-6 (8, 10, 12, 14). Shown in size 4-6.
Intermediate difficulty - Knit, purl, decreases, picking up stitches, working in the round, short rows.

MATERIALS AND NOTIONS

3 (3, 3, 4, 4) skeins of Malabrigo Merino Worsted (100% merino wool; 100g / 210 yds / 192m); #509 Sweet Grape.
US6 (4mm) and US7 (4.5mm) double-pointed and circular needles (24in / 60cm long). Adjust needle size as needed to obtain correct gauge.
Stitch markers in two colors, stitch holders, and tapestry needle.

GAUGE

22 sts and 30 rows = 4in / 10cm in Seeded Rib using larger needles.

STITCH PATTERNS

2x1 Rib (multiple of 3 sts)
Rnd 1: *P1, k1, p1; rep from * to end.
Rep Rnd 1 for patt.

Seeded Rib (multiple of 6 sts)
Rnd 1: *P1, k5; rep from * to end.
Rnd 2: *K5, p1; rep from * to end.
Rep Rnds 1-2 for patt.

BODY

With smaller circular needle, CO 144 (156, 168, 180, 192) sts, pm and join to work in the round. Place a second marker after 72 (78, 84, 90, 96) sts. Work 2x1 Rib for 1½in / 4cm.
Change to larger needle and Seeded Rib and work until piece measures 9½ (11, 12, 13, 13½)in / 24 (28, 30.5, 33, 34.5)cm from cast-on edge, ending with patt Rnd 2.

Next rnd: Work 4 (4, 5, 5, 6) sts, place last 8 (8, 10, 10, 12) sts on a holder, work in patt to 4 (4, 5, 5, 6) sts past next marker, place last 8 (8, 10, 10, 12) sts on a holder, work to end. 64 (70, 74, 80, 84) sts rem for each half of body. Cut yarn and set body aside on circular needle.

SLEEVES

With smaller dpns, CO 42 (42, 48, 48, 48) sts, pm and join to work in the round. Work 2x1 Rib for 1½in / 4cm. Change to larger needles and Seeded Rib. Inc 1 st at the beg and end of next rnd, then every foll 7th (7th, 9th, 9th, 9th) rnd 9 (10, 9, 10, 11) times more. 62 (64, 68, 70, 72) sts.

Work even until sleeve measures 12 (13½, 15, 16½, 17½)in / 30.5 (34.5, 38, 42, 44.5)cm from cast-on edge, ending with patt Rnd 2. Next rnd: Work in patt to 4 (4, 5, 5, 6) sts before marker, place next 8 (8, 10, 10, 12) sts on a holder. 54 (56, 58, 60, 60) sts.

YOKE

Join sleeves and body: Slip 32 (35, 37, 40, 42) front sts onto RH needle without knitting them, pm color A, join yarn. Work 32 (35, 37, 40, 42) rem front sts, pm color B, work 54 (56, 58, 60, 60) sleeve sts, pm color B, work 64 (70, 74, 80, 84) back sts, pm color B, work 54 (56, 58, 60, 60) sleeve sts, pm color B, work 32 (35, 37, 40, 42) front sts to A marker. Rnd now begins at center front.

Shape armholes:
Dec rnd 1: *Work to 2 sts before B marker, ssk, sm, work to next B marker, sm, k2tog; rep from * once more. (4 sts dec'd.)
Rep Dec rnd 1 on every rnd 3 (4, 4, 5, 5) times more. 56 (60, 64, 68, 72) sts each on front and back.

Shape sleeve caps:
Work 1 (2, 2, 2, 2) rnds even.
Dec rnd 2: *Work to B marker, sm, ssk, work to 2 sts before next B marker, k2tog, sm; rep from * once more. (4 sts dec'd.)
Rep Dec rnd 2 on every 3rd rnd 0 (0, 0, 0, 2) times more, then every 2nd rnd 5 (5, 9, 9, 9) times, then every rnd 12

(13, 10, 10, 8) times. 18 (18, 18, 20, 20) sts each sleeve.
Next rnd: Work 6 (6, 7, 7, 8) sts, place last 12 (12, 14, 14, 16) sts just worked on a holder for center front neck. 22 (24, 25, 27, 28) sts rem on each side of front.

Shape right front shoulder and neck:
Row 1 (RS): Work to B marker, sm, ssk, turn.
Row 2 (WS): Sl1, sm, work to 1 st before gap, w&t.
Rep last 2 rows 7 (7, 8, 8, 8) times more. Place rem 15 (17, 17, 19, 20) unwrapped sts on a separate holder; add the 8 (8, 9, 9, 9) wrapped sts to the center front holder.

Shape left front shoulder and neck:
With WS facing, join yarn after center front neck sts on holder.
Row 1 (WS): Work to B marker, sm, p2tog, turn.
Row 2 (RS): Sl1, sm, work in patt to 1 st before gap, w&t.
Rep last 2 rows 7 (7, 8, 8, 8) times more. Place rem 15 (17, 17, 19, 20) unwrapped sts on a separate holder; add the 8 (8, 9, 9, 9) wrapped sts to the center front holder.

Shape back shoulders:
With RS facing, join yarn 1 st before the right back B marker.
Row 1 (RS): Sl1, sm, work to next B marker, sm, ssk, turn.

Row 2 (WS): Sl1, sm, work to next B marker, sm, p2tog, turn.
Rep last 2 rows 7 (7, 8, 8, 8) times more. Leave sts on circular needle and yarn attached.

FINISHING

With right sides facing, join right shoulder with 3-needle bind off, BO 28 (28, 32, 32, 34) center back neck sts, join left shoulder with 3-needle bind off.

Collar:
With RS facing and smaller dpns, pick up and knit 1 st in each st across back neck; knit across 8 (8, 9, 9, 9) sts of left front neck slope, picking up and knitting wraps together with their sts, and increasing 8 (8, 7, 7, 8) sts evenly spaced; work in patt across 12 (12, 14, 14, 16) center front sts; knit across 8 (8, 9, 9, 9) sts of right front neck slope, picking up and knitting wraps together with their sts, and increasing 8 (8, 7, 7, 8) sts evenly spaced; pm. 72 (72, 78, 78, 84) sts. Work in 2x1 Rib for 1in / 2.5cm. BO in patt.

Graft underarms. Weave in ends and block if desired according to the ball band instructions.

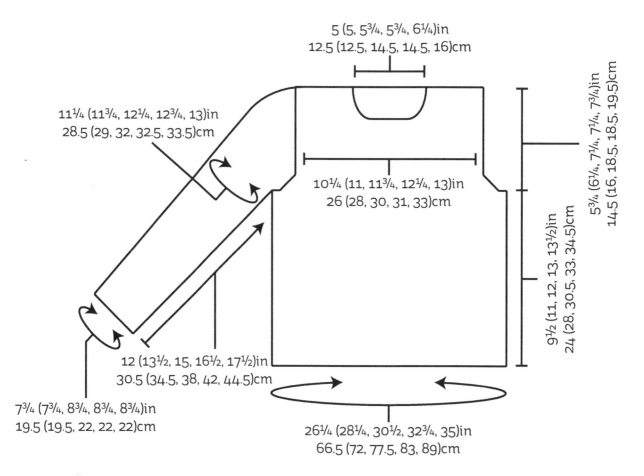

5 (5, 5¾, 5¾, 6¼)in
12.5 (12.5, 14.5, 14.5, 16)cm

11¼ (11¾, 12¼, 12¾, 13)in
28.5 (29, 32, 32.5, 33.5)cm

5¾ (6¼, 7¼, 7¼, 7¾)in
14.5 (16, 18.5, 18.5, 19.5)cm

10¼ (11, 11¾, 12¼, 13)in
26 (28, 30, 31, 33)cm

9½ (11, 12, 13, 13½)in
24 (28, 30.5, 33, 34.5)cm

12 (13½, 15, 16½, 17½)in
30.5 (34.5, 38, 42, 44.5)cm

7¾ (7¾, 8¾, 8¾, 8¾)in
19.5 (19.5, 22, 22, 22)cm

26¼ (28¼, 30½, 32¾, 35)in
66.5 (72, 77.5, 83, 89)cm

DENON

Kashmir Aran is a chainette yarn that seems to work equally well in stockinette and textured knitting, showcasing both beautifully. An intricate mirrored cable running through the center front effortlessly balances the plain knit-and-purl textures.

SIZE & SKILL LEVEL

Finished chest circ - 25½ (27¼, 29¼, 31, 33, 34¾)in / 65 (69, 74.5, 78.5, 84, 88.5) cm. To fit sizes 4 (6, 8, 10, 12, 14). Shown in size 12.
Intermediate difficulty - Knit, purl, cabling, working in the round, short rows, decreases and picking up sts.

MATERIALS AND NOTIONS

10 (11, 11, 12, 13, 13) balls of Louisa Harding Kashmir Aran (55% merino wool, 35% microfiber, 10% cashmere; 50g / 83yds / 75m); #43 Golden.
US7 (4.5mm) and US8 (5mm) double-pointed and circular needles (24in / 60cm long). Adjust needle size as needed to obtain correct gauge.
Stitch markers in two colors, cable needle (cn), stitch holders, and tapestry needle.

GAUGE

17 sts and 23 rnds = 4in / 10cm in St st using larger needles.

STITCH PATTERNS

2x2 Rib (multiple of 4 sts)
Rnd 1: *K2, p2; rep from * to end.
Rep Rnd 1.

(See next page for Cable Panel.)

BODY

With smaller circular needle, CO 108 (116, 124, 132, 140, 148) sts, pm color A and join to work in the rnd. Work in 2x2 Rib for 1½in / 4cm. Change to larger needle.
Set-up rnd 1: P20 (22, 24, 26, 28, 30), pm color B, [k2, m1] twice, k2, p2, [k2, m1] twice, k2, pm color B, p2, knit to end. 112 (120, 128, 136, 144, 152) sts.
Set-up rnd 2: Purl to marker, sm, work Cable Panel over 18 sts, sm, p2, knit to end.

Work as est by last rnd until body measures 9 (10, 11, 12, 13, 13½)in / 23 (25.5, 28, 30.5, 33, 34.5)cm from cast on, ending last rnd 2 sts before the A marker. Do not break yarn.

SLEEVES

With smaller dpns, CO 32 (32, 36, 36, 36, 36) sts, pm color A and join to work in the rnd. Work in 2x2 Rib for 1½in / 4cm. Change to larger needles and St st. Inc 1 st at beg and end of next rnd, then every foll 10th (8h, 10th, 10th, 8th, 8th) rnd 4 (6, 5, 6, 8, 9) times more. 42 (46, 48, 50, 54, 56) sts. Work even until sleeve measures 10½ (11¾, 13, 14¼, 15½, 17)in / 26.5 (30, 33, 36, 39.5, 43)cm from cast on, ending last rnd 2 sts before the marker. Place next 4 sts on a holder for underarm. 38 (42, 44, 46, 50, 52) sts. Break yarn leaving a long tail for grafting underarm.

YOKE

Join body and sleeves: Using circular needle, maintaining st patterns as set throughout yoke, place next 4 body sts on a holder for underarm, k38 (42, 44, 46, 50, 52) sts of first sleeve, pm color A, k1, work across 53 (57, 61, 65, 69, 73) front sts in patt, place next 4 body sts on a holder for underarm, pm color A, k38 (42, 44, 46, 50, 52) sts of second sleeve, pm color A, k50 (54, 58, 62, 66, 70) back sts, pm color A. 180 (196, 208, 220, 236, 248) sts.

Dec rnd 1: *Ssk, work to 2 sts before A marker, k2tog, sm; rep from * 3 times more. (8 sts dec'd.)
Rep Dec Rnd 1 twice more. 48 (52, 56, 60, 64, 68) front sts; 44 (48, 52, 56, 60, 64) back sts; 32 (36, 38, 40, 44, 46) sts each sleeve.
Work 2 rnds even.
Dec rnd 2: *Ssk, work to 2 sts before A marker, k2tog, sm, work to next A marker, sm; rep from * once more. (4 sts dec'd.)
Rep Dec Rnd 2 on every 2nd rnd 2 (4, 5, 6, 8, 9) times, then on every rnd 4 times. 48 (52, 56, 60, 64, 68) front sts; 44 (48, 52, 56, 60, 64) back sts; 18 sts each sleeve.

Shape back shoulders and sleeve caps:
K1 and turn work.
Row 1 (WS): Sl1, sm, work to A marker, sm, p2tog, turn.
Row 2: Sl1, sm, work to A marker, sm, ssk, turn.

Rep Rows 1-2 another 7 times. Place these 46 (50, 54, 58, 62, 66) sts on a holder. Break yarn leaving a long tail for working 3-needle bind off.

Shape front shoulders and sleeve caps:
Join yarn with RS facing, 1 st before the left front A marker.
Row 1 (RS): Sl1, sm, work to A marker, sm, ssk, turn.
Row 2 (WS): Sl1, sm, work to A marker, sm, p2tog, turn.
Rows 3-4: Rep Rows 1-2.
Row 5 (RS): Sl1, sm, work 15 (17, 18, 20, 21, 23) sts, BO center 18 (18, 20, 20, 22, 22) sts, work to A marker, sm, ssk, turn.

Right front neck:
Row 1 and all WS rows: Sl1, sm, work to end.
Row 2 (RS): BO 2 sts, work to A marker, sm, ssk, turn.
Row 4: BO 1 st, work to A marker, sm, ssk, turn.
Row 6: Rep Row 4.
Row 8: Work to A marker, sm, ssk, turn.
Row 10: Rep Row 8.

Left front neck:
Join yarn at neck edge with WS facing.
Row 1 (WS): BO 2 sts, work to A marker, sm, p2tog, turn.
Row 2 and all RS rows: Sl1, sm, work to end.
Row 3: BO 1 st, work to A marker, sm, p2tog, turn.
Row 5: Rep Row 3.
Row 7: Work to A marker, sm, p2tog, turn.
Row 9: Rep Row 7.
Row 10: Sl1, sm, work to end. Place these 12 (14, 15, 17, 18, 20) sts on a holder.

FINISHING

With right sides facing, join right shoulder using 3-needle bind off, BO next 22 (22, 24, 24, 26, 26) sts for back neck, join left shoulder using a 3-needle bind off.

[Instructions continue on next page.]

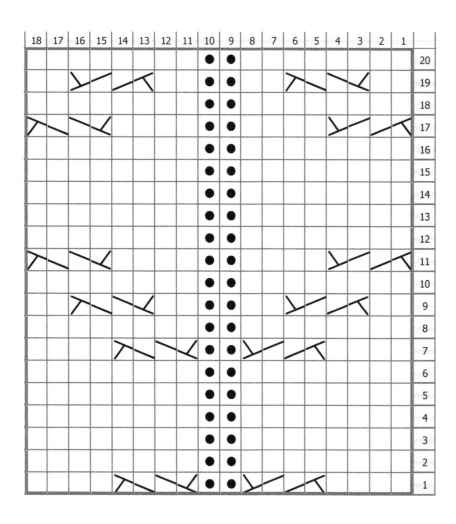

Cable Panel
(worked over 18 sts)

Rnd 1: K4, C4R, p2, C4L, k4.
Rnds 2-6: K8, p2, k8.
Rnd 7: K4, C4R, p2, C4L, k4.
Rnd 8: K8, p2, k8.
Rnd 9: K2, C4R, k2, p2, k2, C4L, k2.
Rnd 10: K8, p2, k8.
Rnd 11: C4R, k4, p2, k4, C4L.
Rnds 12-16: K8, p2, k8.
Rnd 17: C4R, k4, p2, k4, C4L.
Rnd 18: K8, p2, k8.
Rnd 19: K2, C4L, k2, p2, k2, C4R, k2.
Rnd 20: K8, p2, k8.
Rep Rnds 1-20.

C4R: Sl 2 to cn and hold to back, k2, k2 from cn.
C4L: Sl 2 to cn and hold to front, k2, k2 from cn.

HOOD

With RS facing, using larger circular needle and beg in the center of the front cable panel, pick up and knit 15 (15, 16, 16, 17, 17) sts along right front neck edge, 11 (11, 12, 12, 13, 13) sts to center back neck, pm, 11 (11, 12, 12, 13, 13) sts along remainder of back neck, and 15 (15, 16, 16, 17, 17) sts down left front neck. 52 (52, 56, 56, 60, 60) sts.

Next row (WS): K4, purl to marker increasing 11 (13, 13, 15, 15, 17) sts evenly spaced, sm, purl to last 4 sts increasing 11 (13, 13, 15, 15, 17) sts evenly spaced, k4. 74 (78, 82, 86, 90, 94) sts.

Keeping 4 sts at each edge in garter st and working remainder of hood in St st, work even until hood measures 6 (6½, 7, 7½, 8, 8½)in / 15 (16.5, 18, 19, 20.5, 21.5)cm from pick-up row.

Shape top:
Dec row 1 (RS): Knit to 2 sts before marker, ssk, sm, k2tog, knit to end. (2 sts dec'd.)
Rep Dec Row 1 on every 4th row once more, then on every 2nd row 7 times. 56 (60, 64, 68, 72, 76) sts.
Dec row 2 (WS): K4, purl to 2 sts before marker, p2tog, sm, ssp, purl to last 4 sts, k4. (2 sts dec'd.)
Rep Dec Rows 1-2 twice more. 46 (50, 54, 58, 62, 66) sts.
Divide hood sts over 2 needles. With right sides facing, join with a 3-needle bind off.

Weave in all ends, graft underarm sts together and block if desired according to the ball band instructions.

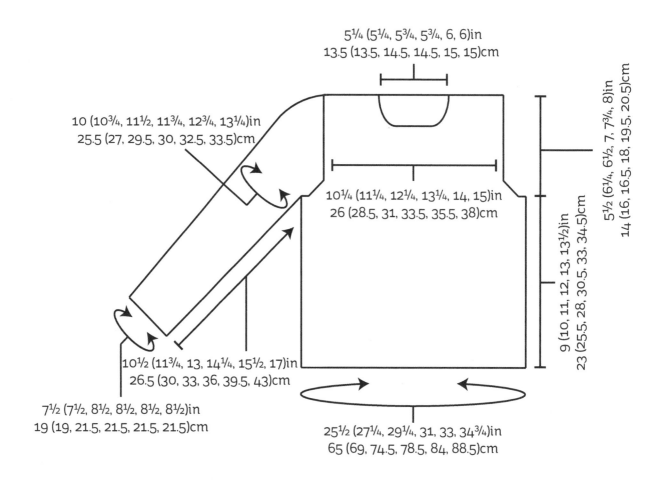

5¼ (5¼, 5¾, 5¾, 6, 6)in
13.5 (13.5, 14.5, 14.5, 15, 15)cm

10 (10¾, 11½, 11¾, 12¾, 13¼)in
25.5 (27, 29.5, 30, 32.5, 33.5)cm

10¼ (11¼, 12¼, 13¼, 14, 15)in
26 (28.5, 31, 33.5, 35.5, 38)cm

5½ (6¼, 6½, 7, 7¾, 8)in
14 (16, 16.5, 18, 19.5, 20.5)cm

9 (10, 11, 12, 13, 13½)in
23 (25.5, 28, 30.5, 33, 34.5)cm

10½ (11¾, 13, 14¼, 15½, 17)in
26.5 (30, 33, 36, 39.5, 43)cm

7½ (7½, 8½, 8½, 8½, 8½)in
19 (19, 21.5, 21.5, 21.5, 21.5)cm

25½ (27¼, 29¼, 31, 33, 34¾)in
65 (69, 74.5, 78.5, 84, 88.5)cm

ELDON

This classic cabled, v-neck vest starts with a wide rib at the hem that moves organically into the cable pattern. The cable is then worked continuously to armholes. At the armholes, the body is separated into front and back and the armhole and collar trims are worked after the shoulders have been joined.

SIZE & SKILL LEVEL

Finished chest circ - 26¼ (28¼, 30, 31¾, 33¾)in / 66.5 (72, 76, 80.5, 85.5)cm. To fit sizes 4-6 (8, 10, 12, 14). Shown in size 12.
Intermediate difficulty - Knit, purl, working in the round, decreases and picking up sts.

MATERIALS AND NOTIONS

3 (3, 3, 3, 4) skeins of Lorna's Laces Shepherd Worsted (100% superwash merino wool; 113g / 225 yds / 205m); Pewter.
US7 (4.5mm) and US8 (5mm) circular needles (24in / 60cm long). Adjust needle size as needed to obtain correct gauge.
US 7 (4.5mm) double-pointed needles.
Stitch markers, stitch holders, cable needle (cn), and tapestry needle.

GAUGE

24 sts = 3¾in / 9.5cm and 24 rows = 3½in / 9cm in Cable patt using larger needles.

STITCH PATTERNS

5x4 Rib (multiple of 9 sts)
Rnd 1: *K2, p5, k2; rep from * to end.
Rep Rnd 1 for patt.

2x2 Rib (multiple of 4 sts)
Rnd 1: *K2, p2; rep from * to end.
Rep Rnd 1 for patt.

(See next page for Cable patt.)

PATTERN NOTES

When binding off over cable patt, work k2tog/p2tog as appropriate above each cable to avoid puckering.

BODY

With smaller circular needle, CO 126 (135, 144, 153, 162) sts, pm and join to work in the round. Work in 5x4 Rib for 1½in / 4cm.
Change to larger needle. Inc rnd: *K2, p1, [pfb] 3 times, p1, k2; rep from * to end. 168 (180, 192, 204, 216) sts. Place a second marker after 84 (90, 96, 102, 108) sts.
Work in Cable patt until body measures 10 (11, 12, 13, 13½) in / 25.5 (28, 30.5, 33, 34.5)cm from cast-on edge, ending with an odd-numbered rnd.

Divide for armholes:
Next rnd: *Work in patt to 3 (0, 3, 0, 3) sts before next marker, BO 6 sts; rep from * once more. 78 (84, 90, 96, 102) sts each on front and back.
Note: As sts are decreased away at the armholes and the neckline, work in patt over a whole or half cable repeat only (i.e. do not work partial cables). Keep remaining sts along the edge in reverse St st, with the last edge stitch in St st for ease of finishing.

UPPER BACK

Dec row 1 (RS): K1, k3tog, work in patt to last 4 sts, sssk, k1. (4 sts dec'd.)
Work 1 WS row even.
Rep last 2 rows once more. 70 (76, 82, 88, 94) sts.
Dec row 2 (RS): K1, k2tog, work in patt to last 3 sts, ssk, k1. (2 sts dec'd.)
Work 1 WS row even.
Rep last 2 rows twice more. 64 (70, 76, 82, 88) sts. **
Work even until armhole measures 6 (6½, 7, 7½, 8)in / 15 (16.5, 18, 19, 20.5)cm, ending with a WS row.
Next row (RS): Work 14 (16, 18, 20, 22) sts, BO 36 (38, 40, 42, 44) sts, work rem 14 (16, 18, 20, 22) sts. Place sts on holders.

UPPER FRONT

Join yarn with RS facing and work armhole shaping as for back to **.
Work even until armholes measure 1½ (1½, 1¾, 2, 2¼)in / 4 (4, 4.5, 5, 5.5)cm, ending with a WS row.
Next row (RS): Work 29 (32, 35, 37, 40) sts, BO 6 (6, 6, 8, 8) sts, work rem 29 (32, 35, 37, 40) sts.

Right neck and shoulder:
Work 1 WS row even.
Dec row (RS): K1, k2tog, work in patt to last st, k1. (1 st dec'd.)
Rep Dec row on every 2nd row 14 (15, 16, 15, 16) times more, then on every 4th row 0 (0, 0, 1, 1) times. 14 (16, 18, 20, 22) sts.
Work even until armhole measures same as back to shoulder. Place sts on holder.

Left neck and shoulder:
Join yarn at neck edge and work 1 WS row even.
Dec row (RS): K1, work in patt to last st, ssk, k1. (1 st dec'd.)
Rep Dec row on every 2nd row 14 (15, 16, 15, 16) times more, then on every 4th row 0 (0, 0, 1, 1) times. 14 (16, 18, 20, 22) sts.
Work even until armhole measures same as back to shoulder. Place sts on holder.

FINISHING
Join shoulders using a 3-needle bind off.

Collar
With smaller circular needle, RS facing, pick up and knit 1 st in every st and 3 sts for every 4 rows up the right front neck, across back neck, and down left front neck sts. Do not pick up sts along the center front bind off, and do not join. Adjust st count as necessary to achieve a multiple of 4. Work in 2x2 Rib for 1 (1, 1, 1¼, 1¼)in / 2.5 (2.5, 2.5, 3, 3)cm. BO in patt. Sew short edges of collar to the center front bind off, with right side overlapping the left.

Armhole edging
With dpns, RS facing, and starting in the middle of underarm bind off, pick up and knit 1 st in every st and 3 sts for every 4 rows around armhole. Adjust st count as necessary to achieve a multiple of 4. Join to work in the round. Work in 2x2 Rib for 1in / 2.5 cm. BO in patt.

Weave in ends and block according to ball band instructions.

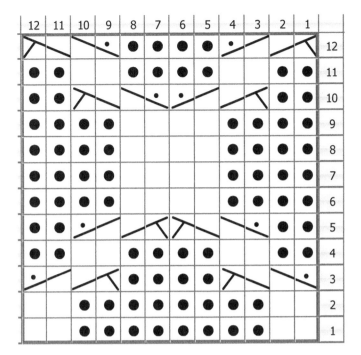

Cable Pattern

(multiple of 12 sts)

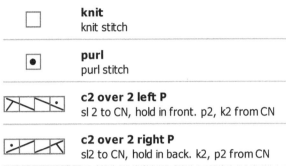

	knit
	knit stitch

	purl
●	purl stitch

	c2 over 2 left P
	sl 2 to CN, hold in front. p2, k2 from CN

	c2 over 2 right P
	sl2 to CN, hold in back. k2, p2 from CN

Rnd 1: *K2, p8, k2; rep from * to end.
Rnd 2 and all even rnds: Work each st as it presents itself (knit the knits and purl the purls).
Rnd 3: *T4L (sl 2 to cn and hold to front, p2, k2 from cn), p4, T4R (sl 2 to cn and hold to back, k2, p2 from cn); rep from * to end.
Rnd 5: *P2, T4L, T4R, p2; rep from * to end.
Rnd 7: *P4, k4, p4; rep from * to end.
Rnd 9: *P2, T4R, T4L, p2; rep from * to end.
Rnd 11: *T4R, p4, T4L; rep from * to end.
Rnd 12: Work each st as it presents itself.
Rep Rnds 1–12 for patt.

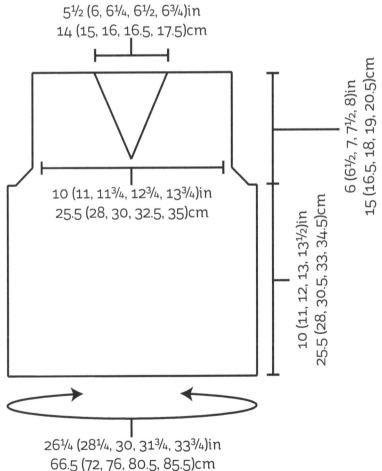

5½ (6, 6¼, 6½, 6¾)in
14 (15, 16, 16.5, 17.5)cm

10 (11, 11¾, 12¾, 13¾)in
25.5 (28, 30, 32.5, 35)cm

6 (6½, 7, 7½, 8)in
15 (16.5, 18, 19, 20.5)cm

10 (11, 12, 13, 13½)in
25.5 (28, 30.5, 33, 34.5)cm

26¼ (28¼, 30, 31¾, 33¾)in
66.5 (72, 76, 80.5, 85.5)cm

TRANTOR

Trantor is a saddle-shouldered sweater with a short funnel neck. The dash pattern on the body was inspired by the beautiful faint streaks created on the fabric by Lorna's Laces' semi-solid yarn. And the two harmonize so well together.

SIZE & SKILL LEVEL

Finished chest circ - 25¼ (29½, 33¾)in / 64 (75, 85.5)cm. To fit sizes 4-6 (8-10, 12-14). Shown in size 8-10. Intermediate difficulty - Knit, purl, working in the round, decreases and picking up sts.

MATERIALS AND NOTIONS

3 (4, 4) skeins of Lorna's Laces Shepherd Worsted (100% superwash merino wool; 4oz / 225yds / 205m); Patina. US7 (4.5mm) and US8 (5mm) double-pointed and circular needles (24in / 60cm long). Adjust needle size as needed to obtain correct gauge.
Stitch markers, stitch holders, and tapestry needle.

GAUGE

19 sts and 24 rnds = 4in / 10cm over Dash patt and St st using larger needles.

STITCH PATTERNS

Alternating rib (multiple of 4 sts)
Rnd 1: *K2, p2; rep from * to end.
Rnd 2: *P2, k2; rep from * to end.
Rep Rnds 1-2 for patt.

(See next page for Dash Pattern.)

BODY

With smaller circular needle, CO 120 (140, 160) sts, pm and join to work in the round. Place a second marker after 60 (70, 80) sts.
Work in Alternating Rib for 1½in / 4cm.

Change to larger needle and work in Dash patt until body measures 10 (11½, 13)in / 25.5 (29, 33)cm from cast-on edge.
Next rnd: Work 3 sts, place the last 6 sts on a holder, work to 3 sts past second marker, place the last 6 sts on

a holder, work to end. 54 (64, 74) sts rem for each half of body. Leave sts on circular needle with yarn attached.

SLEEVES

With smaller dpns CO 36 (40, 44) sts, pm and join to work in the round. Work in Alternating Rib for 1½in / 4cm. Change to larger needles and St st. Inc 1 st at beg and end of next rnd, then every foll 8th rnd 5 (7, 9) times more. 48 (56, 64) sts. Work even until sleeve measures 11 (14, 16)in / 28 (35.5, 40.5)cm from cast-on edge, ending last rnd 3 sts before the marker. Place next 6 sts on a holder. 42 (50, 58) sts rem.

YOKE

Join body and sleeves: With circular needle and yarn attached to body, *knit 42 (50, 58) sleeve sts, pm, work in patt over 54 (64, 74) half body sts, pm; rep from * once more. Rnd now begins on the front, just before the right sleeve.

Shape armholes:
Dec rnd 1: *Ssk, work to 2 sts before next marker, k2tog, sm; rep from * 3 times more. (8 sts dec'd.)
Rep Dec rnd 1 on every 2nd rnd twice more. 48 (58, 68) sts rem on front and back, 36 (44, 52) sts in each sleeve.
Dec rnd 2: *Ssk, work to 2 sts before next marker, k2tog, sm, work to next marker, sm; rep from * once more. (4 sts dec'd.)
Rep Dec rnd 2 on every 2nd rnd 9 (12, 15) times more. 16 (18, 20) sts in each sleeve.
Next rnd: Work across right sleeve, back, and left sleeve sts to 3rd marker, sm. Cut yarn. Sl next 15 (19, 23) sts to RH needle without knitting them. Place following 18 (20, 22) center front sts on a holder. Join yarn after the held sts with RS facing and cont working back and forth to shape saddles and neck.

Shape front neck:
Row 1 (RS): K2, ssk, *work to 2 sts before marker, k2tog, sm, ssk; rep from * 3 times more, work to last 4 sts, k2tog, k2. (10 sts dec'd.)
Row 2 (WS): *Work to 2 sts before marker, ssp, sm, p2tog; rep from * 3 more times, work to end. (8 sts dec'd.)
Rep Rows 1-2 once more. 9 (13, 17) sts each side of front, 8 (10, 12) sts each sleeve, 40 (50, 60) back sts. Cut yarn.

Shape back neck:
With RS facing, sl 9 (13, 17) right front sts to RH needle and remove the first marker. Join yarn. As you work the first row, remove existing markers as you come to them and replace where indicated.
Row 1 (RS): Sl1, pm, k6 (8, 10), pm, ssk, work across back sts to 1 st before marker, k2tog, pm, k6 (8, 10), pm, ssk, turn.
Row 2 (WS): Sl1, sm, purl to last marker, sm, p2tog, turn.
Row 3: Sl1, sm, knit to marker, sm, ssk, work to 2 sts before next marker, k2tog, sm, k to marker, sm, ssk, turn.
Row 4: Sl1, sm, purl to last marker, sm, p2tog, turn.
7 (11, 15) sts each side of front, 6 (8, 10) sts each sleeve, 36 (46, 56) back sts.

**Shape saddle:
Row 1 (RS): Sl1, sm, k to marker, sm, ssk, turn.
Row 2 (WS): Sl1, sm, purl to marker, sm, p2tog, turn.
Rep Rows 1-2 another 5 (9, 13) times, until 1 st rem in front section.**
Next row (RS): Sl1, sm, k to next marker, sm, ssk, BO next 20 (22, 24) sts for back neck, work to 1 st before next marker. Rep from ** to ** for second saddle.

FINISHING

Collar
With smaller dpns, knit across sts of left saddle, pick up and knit 3 sts for every 4 rows down left front neck edge, knit across the center front sts from the holder, pick up and knit 3 sts for every 4 rows up right side of neck, knit across saddle sts, pick up and knit 1 st in each st across back neck, pm. Count sts and adjust to a multiple of 4 on next rnd if needed. Work Alternating Rib for 1in / 2.5cm. BO loosely in patt.

Graft underarm stitches. Weave in ends. Block according to ball band directions.

Dash Pattern

10	9	8	7	6	5	4	3	2	1	
		●	●	●	●	●	●			8
										7
										6
										5
●	●	●					●	●	●	4
										3
										2
										1

☐ **knit**

⊡ **purl**

(Multiple of 10 sts.)
Rnds 1-3: Knit.
Rnd 4: *P3, k4, p3; rep from * to end.
Rnds 5-7: Knit.
Rnd 8: *K2, p6, k2; rep from * to end.
Rep Rnds 1-8 for patt.

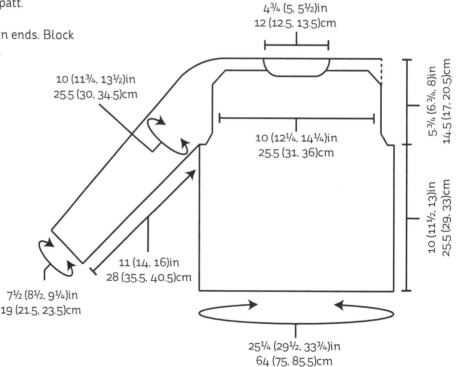

4¾ (5, 5½)in
12 (12.5, 13.5)cm

10 (11¾, 13½)in
25.5 (30, 34.5)cm

5¾ (6¾, 8)in
14.5 (17, 20.5)cm

10 (12¼, 14¼)in
25.5 (31, 36)cm

11 (14, 16)in
28 (35.5, 40.5)cm

10 (11½, 13)in
25.5 (29, 33)cm

7½ (8½, 9¼)in
19 (21.5, 23.5)cm

25¼ (29½, 33¾)in
64 (75, 85.5)cm

DECKARD

This zippered raglan cardigan with a hood is worked from the bottom seamlessly to the armholes, where the sleeves are joined with the body. Sleeve shaping is worked on the outer side of the sleeve.

SIZE & SKILL LEVEL

Finished chest circ - 28 (29¼, 30¾, 32, 34, 36)in / 71 (74.5, 78, 81.5, 86.5, 91.5)cm, zipped. To fit sizes 4 (6, 8, 10, 12, 14). Shown in size 10 (sleeved version) & size 12 (vest).
Easy difficulty - Knit, purl, raglan shaping, picking up stitches, working in the round.

MATERIALS AND NOTIONS

Malabrigo Chunky (100% merino wool; 100g / 104yds / 95m); #259 Charrua.
- 5 (5, 6, 6, 6, 7) skeins for sleeved version
- 4 (4, 4, 5, 5, 5) skeins for vest version

US10½ (6.5 mm) double-pointed and circular needles (32in / 80cm long). Adjust needle size as needed to obtain correct gauge.
Separating zipper:
- Approx 14 (15½, 17, 18½, 19½, 20½)in / 35.5 (39.5, 43, 47, 49.5, 52)cm long for sleeved version
- Approx 12½ (14, 15½, 17, 18½, 19½)in / 32 (35.5, 39.5, 43, 47, 49.5)cm for vest version

Stitch markers in two colors, stitch holders, tapestry needle, sewing needle, and thread.

GAUGE

12 sts and 18 rows = 4in / 10 cm in St st.

BODY

With circular needle, CO 84 (88, 92, 96, 102, 108) sts.
Work in garter st for 2in / 5cm.
Next row (RS): Knit.
Next row (WS): K4, purl to last 4 sts, k4.

Cont working in St st with 4 sts in garter st at each edge until body measures 9 (10, 11, 12, 13, 13½)in / 23 (25.5, 28, 30.5, 33, 34.5)cm from cast on, ending with a WS row. Leave sts on circular ndl while you work sleeves.

SLEEVES

With dpns CO 24 (24, 26, 26, 28, 28) sts, pm color A and join for working in the rnd. Work in garter st (knit and purl alternate rnds) for 2in / 5cm, ending with a knit rnd.
Set up sleeve patt: K10 (10, 11, 11, 12, 12), pm color B, p4, pm color B, k10 (10, 11, 11, 12, 12).
Cont working sleeve in St st with 4 sts in reverse St st between the markers.
Inc rnd: Knit to B marker, m1R, sm, p4, sm, m1L, knit to end. 2 sts inc'd.
Rep Inc rnd on every foll 8th rnd 4 (5, 4, 5, 5, 6) times more. 34 (36, 36, 38, 40, 42) sts. Work even until sleeve measures 10½ (11¾, 13, 14¼, 15½, 17)in / 26.5 (30, 33, 36, 39.5, 43)cm from cast on, ending last rnd 2 sts before the beg-of-rnd marker. Place next 4 sts on a holder. 30 (32, 32, 34, 36, 38) sts. Break yarn leaving a long tail for grafting underarm.

YOKE

Join sleeves and body: With circular ndl and RS facing, maintaining est st patterns on body and sleeves, k19 (20, 21, 22, 23, 25) right front sts, place next 4 sts on holder for underarm, pm color A, work 30 (32, 32, 34, 36, 38) sleeve sts, pm color A, k38 (40, 42, 44, 48, 50) back sts, place next 4 sts on holder for underarm, pm color A, work 30 (32, 32, 34, 36, 38) sleeve sts, pm color A, k19 (20, 21, 22, 23, 25) left front sts. 136 (144, 148, 156, 166, 176) sts.
Work 1 (1, 3, 3, 3, 3) rows even.
Raglan dec row (RS): *Work to 3 sts before A marker, ssk, k1, sm, k1, k2tog; rep from * 3 times more, work to end. (8 sts dec'd.)
Rep Raglan Dec Row on every RS row 9 (10, 10, 11, 12, 13) times more. 56 (56, 60, 60, 62, 64) sts total. 9 (9, 10, 10, 10, 11) sts each front; 10 sleeve sts; 18 (18, 20, 20, 22, 22) back sts.
Work 1 WS row even.

Shape neck:
Row 1 (RS): K4, place sts just worked on a holder, *work to 3 sts before A marker, ssk, k1, sm, k1, k2tog; rep from * 3 times more, work to end.
Row 2 (WS): K4, place sts just worked on a holder, work to end. 4 (4, 5, 5, 5, 6) sts each front; 8 sleeve sts; 16 (16, 18, 18, 20, 20) back sts.

SIZES 4 & 6 ONLY:
Row 3: Work Raglan Dec Row.
Row 4: Work even.
Row 5: *Work to 3 sts before A marker, ssk, k1, sm, ssk, p2, k2tog, sm, k1, k2tog; rep from * once more, work to end. 24 sts rem.
BO all sts.

SIZES 8 , 10, & 12 ONLY:
Row 3: Work Raglan Dec Row.
Row 4: Work even.
Row 5: Sl1, k2tog, psso, k1, sm, k1, ssk, p2, k2tog, sm, k1, k2tog, work to 3 sts before A marker, ssk, k1, sm, ssk, p2, k2tog, sm, k1, k3tog. 26 (26, 28) sts rem.
BO all sts.

SIZE 14 ONLY:
Row 3: Ssk, *work to 3 sts before A marker, ssk, k1, sm, k1, k2tog; rep from * 3 times more, work to last 2 sts, k2tog.
Row 4: Work even.
Row 5: Sl1, k2tog, psso, k1, sm, k1, ssk, p2, k2tog, sm, k1, k2tog, work to 3 sts before A marker, ssk, k1, sm, ssk, p2, k2tog, sm, k1, k3tog. 28 sts rem.
BO all sts.

HOOD

With circular ndl and RS facing, p4 from right neck holder, pick up and knit 26 (26, 28, 28, 30, 30) sts around neck, k4 from left neck holder. 34 (34, 36, 36, 38, 38) sts.
Next row (WS): K4, purl to end.
Hood inc row (RS): P4, knit to last 4 sts increasing 9 (10, 10, 11, 11, 12) sts evenly spaced, k4.
Rep last 2 rows once more. 52 (54, 56, 58, 60, 62) sts. Pm after 26 (27, 28, 29, 30, 31) sts to divide hood in half.
Work even, keeping 4 sts in garter st at each edge, until hood measures 6½ (7, 7, 7½, 8, 8)in / 16.5 (18, 18, 19.5, 20.5, 20.5)cm from pick-up row, ending with a WS row.

Shape top:
Hood dec row 1 (RS): Work to 2 sts before m, ssk, sm, k2tog, work to end. (2 sts dec'd.)
Rep Hood dec row 1 on every 4th row once more, then on every 2nd row 5 times. 38 (40, 42, 44, 46, 48) sts.
Hood dec row 2 (WS): Work to 2 sts before marker, p2tog, sm, ssp, work to end. (2 sts dec'd.)
Work Hood dec rows 1 and 2 once more. 32 (34, 36, 38, 40, 42) sts.
Place sts on either side of marker onto separate needles, right sides facing, and join using a 3-needle bind off.

FINISHING

Graft underarm sts together, weave in all ends and block if desired according to ball band instructions. Sew in the zipper.

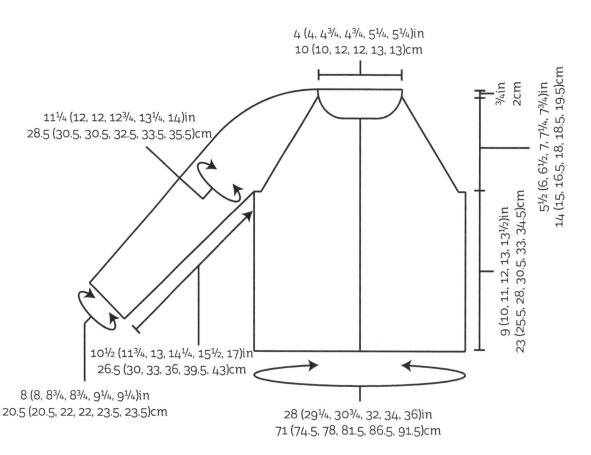

4 (4, 4¾, 4¾, 5¼, 5¼)in
10 (10, 12, 12, 13, 13)cm

11¼ (12, 12, 12¾, 13¼, 14)in
28.5 (30.5, 30.5, 32.5, 33.5, 35.5)cm

¾in
2cm

5½ (6, 6½, 7, 7¼, 7¾)in
14 (15, 16.5, 18, 18.5, 19.5)cm

9 (10, 11, 12, 13, 13½)in
23 (25.5, 28, 30.5, 33, 34.5)cm

10½ (11¾, 13, 14¼, 15½, 17)in
26.5 (30, 33, 36, 39.5, 43)cm

8 (8, 8¾, 8¾, 9¼, 9¼)in
20.5 (20.5, 22, 22, 23.5, 23.5)cm

28 (29¼, 30¾, 32, 34, 36)in
71 (74.5, 78, 81.5, 86.5, 91.5)cm

MAKE IT A VEST

For the best fit, this vest version of the Deckard hoodie has a fitted rather than raglan armhole.

BODY

With circular needle, CO 84 (88, 92, 96, 102, 108) sts. Work in garter st for 2in / 5cm.
Next row (RS): Knit.
Next row (WS): K4, purl to last 4 sts, k4.
Cont working in St st with 4 sts in garter st at each edge until body measures 8 (9, 10, 11, 12, 12½)in / 20.5 (23, 25.5, 28, 30.5, 32)cm from cast on, ending with WS row.
Next row (RS): K17 (18, 19, 20, 21, 23) right front sts, pm, k8 (8, 8, 8, 9, 8), pm, k34 (36, 38, 40, 42, 46) back sts, pm, k8 (8, 8, 8, 9, 8), pm, k17 (18, 19, 20, 21, 23) left front sts.
Next row (WS): K4, (purl to m, sm, knit to m, sm) twice, purl to last 4 sts, k4.
Cont in St st with 4 sts at each edge and 8 (8, 8, 8, 9, 8) sts at each underarm in garter st for 2 more rows.

Divide back and front (RS): K19 (20, 21, 22, 23, 25) right front sts, BO 4 (4, 4, 4, 5, 4) sts, k38 (40, 42, 44, 46, 50) back sts, BO 4 (4, 4, 4, 5, 4) sts, k19 (20, 21, 22, 23, 25) left front sts.

UPPER LEFT FRONT

Next row (WS): K4, purl to last 4 sts, k4.
Armhole dec row (RS): K4, k2tog, knit to end. (1 st dec'd.)
Rep these 2 rows twice more. 16 (17, 18, 19, 20, 22) sts.
Work even, keeping 4 sts in garter st at each edge, until armhole measures 3½ (4, 4½, 5, 5½, 5½)in / 9 (10, 11.5, 12.5, 14, 14)cm, ending with a RS row.

Shape neck:
Next row (WS): K4, place these 4 sts on a holder, purl to last 4 sts, k4. 12 (13, 14, 15, 16, 18) sts.
Neck dec row (RS): Knit to last 3 sts, ssk, k1. (1 st dec'd.)
Next row: Sl1, purl to last 4 sts, k4.
Rep last 2 rows 1 (1, 2, 2, 2, 3) times more. 10 (11, 11, 12, 13, 14) sts. Work even until armhole measures 5½ (6, 6½, 7, 7½, 8)in / 14 (15, 16.5, 18, 19, 20.5) cm. Place sts on holder.

UPPER BACK

Join yarn to 38 (40, 42, 44, 46, 50) back sts with WS facing.
Next row (WS): K4, purl to last 4 sts, k4.
Armhole dec row (RS): K4, k2tog, knit to last 6 sts, ssk, k4. (2 sts dec'd.)
Rep last 2 rows twice more. 32 (34, 36, 38, 40, 44) sts.

Work even, keeping 4 sts in garter st at each edge, until armhole measures 5½ (6, 6½, 7, 7½, 8)in / 14 (15, 16.5, 18, 19, 20.5) cm. Place sts on holder.

UPPER RIGHT FRONT

Join yarn to rem 19 (20, 21, 22, 23, 25) sts with WS facing.
Next row (WS): K4, purl to last 4 sts, k4.
Armhole dec row (RS): Knit to last 6 sts, ssk, k4. (1 st dec'd.)
Rep these 2 rows twice more. 16 (17, 18, 19, 20, 22) sts.
Work even, keeping 4 sts in garter st at each edge, until armhole measures 3½ (4, 4½, 5, 5½, 5½)in / 9 (10, 11.5, 12.5, 14, 14)cm, ending with a WS row.

Shape neck:
Next row (RS): K4 and place these sts on a holder, knit to end.
Next row (WS): K4, purl to end.
Neck dec row: Sl1, k2tog, knit to end. (1 st dec'd.)
Rep last 2 rows 1 (1, 2, 2, 2, 3) times more. 10 (11, 11, 12, 13, 14) sts. Work even until armhole measures 5½ (6, 6½, 7, 7½, 8)in / 14 (15, 16.5, 18, 19, 20.5) cm, ending with a RS row.

FINISHING

Starting at right armhole edge, using yarn attached to right front, join right shoulder sts using a 3-needle bind off, BO 12 (12, 14, 14, 14, 16) back neck sts, join left shoulder sts with 3-needle bind off. Work Hood as for jacket (see page 62). Weave in all ends, block if desired according to ball band instructions and sew in zipper.

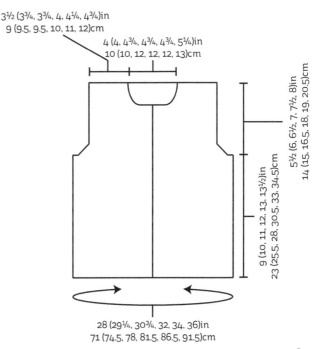

3½ (3¾, 3¾, 4, 4¼, 4¾)in
9 (9.5, 9.5, 10, 11, 12)cm

4 (4, 4¾, 4¾, 4¾, 5¼)in
10 (10, 12, 12, 12, 13)cm

5½ (6, 6½, 7, 7½, 8)in
14 (15, 16.5, 18, 19, 20.5)cm

9 (10, 11, 12, 13, 13½)in
23 (25.5, 28, 30.5, 33, 34.5)cm

28 (29¼, 30¾, 32, 34, 36)in
71 (74.5, 78, 81.5, 86.5, 91.5)cm

RUNAROUND

This sweater's richly textured knit-and-purl pattern perfectly highlights its circular yoke. The yoke shaping is incorporated into the stitch pattern all the way through.

SIZE & SKILL LEVEL

Finished chest circ - 25½ (29, 32¾)in / 65 (73.5, 83)cm. To fit sizes 4 (6-8, 10-12). Shown in size 6-8.
Intermediate difficulty - Knit, purl, decreases, picking up stitches, working in the round.

MATERIALS AND NOTIONS

7 (8, 9) balls of Debbie Bliss Rialto DK (100% superwash merino wool; 50g / 114 yds / 105m); #23038 gray.
US5 (3.75mm) and US6 (4mm) double-pointed and circular needles (24in / 60cm long). Adjust needle size as needed to obtain correct gauge.
Stitch marker, stitch holders, and tapestry needle.

GAUGE

22 sts and 30 rnds = 4in / 10cm in St st using larger needles.
22 sts and 32 rnds = 4in / 10cm in Main Chart patt using larger needles, measured unstretched.

STITCH PATTERNS

Hem Rib (multiple of 10 sts):
Rnd 1: *[P2, k2] twice, p2; rep from * to end.
Rep Rnd 1.

2x1 Rib (multiple of 3 sts):
Rnd 1: *K2, p1; rep from * to end.
Rep Rnd 1.

(See pages 68-69 for Charts.)

BODY

With smaller circular needle, CO 140 (160, 180) sts, pm and join to work in the round. Work Hem Rib for 1½in / 4cm.

Change to larger needle. Work Main Chart until body measures approx 9 (10¼, 12¾)in / 23 (26, 32.5)cm from cast on, ending with Rnd 20 (10, 10) of patt. Stop working last rnd 5 sts before marker. Do not break yarn.

SLEEVES

With smaller dpns, CO 40 (50, 50) sts, pm and join to work in the round. Work Hem Rib for 2½ (1½, 1½)in / 6.5 (4, 4)cm.

Change to larger needles and work following Main Chart. Inc 1 st at beg and end of next rnd, then every foll 6th (8th, 10th) rnd 9 times more. 60 (70, 70) sts.

Work even until sleeve measures approx 10 (12¾, 15¼) in / 25.5 (32.5, 38.5)cm from cast on, ending with Rnd 20 (10, 10) of patt. Stop working last rnd 5 sts before the marker. Place next 10 sts on a holder for underarm. 50 (60, 60) sts rem. Cut yarn leaving a long tail for grafting underarm.

YOKE

Join body and sleeves on circular needle as foll: Place next 10 body sts on a holder for underarm. Work 50 (60, 60) sts of left sleeve in patt, work 60 (70, 80) body sts in patt, place next 10 body sts on a holder, work 50 (60, 60) sts of right sleeve in patt, work rem 60 (70, 80) body sts in patt, pm for beg of rnd. 220 (260, 280) sts.

Work 9 rnds even, ending with Rnd 10 (20, 20) of main patt.
Work Yoke Chart for your size. 66 (78, 84) sts rem.

COLLAR

Work in 2x1 Rib for 1¼in / 2cm. BO loosely in patt.

FINISHING

Graft underarms closed. Weave in ends and block according to ball band instructions.

Main Chart

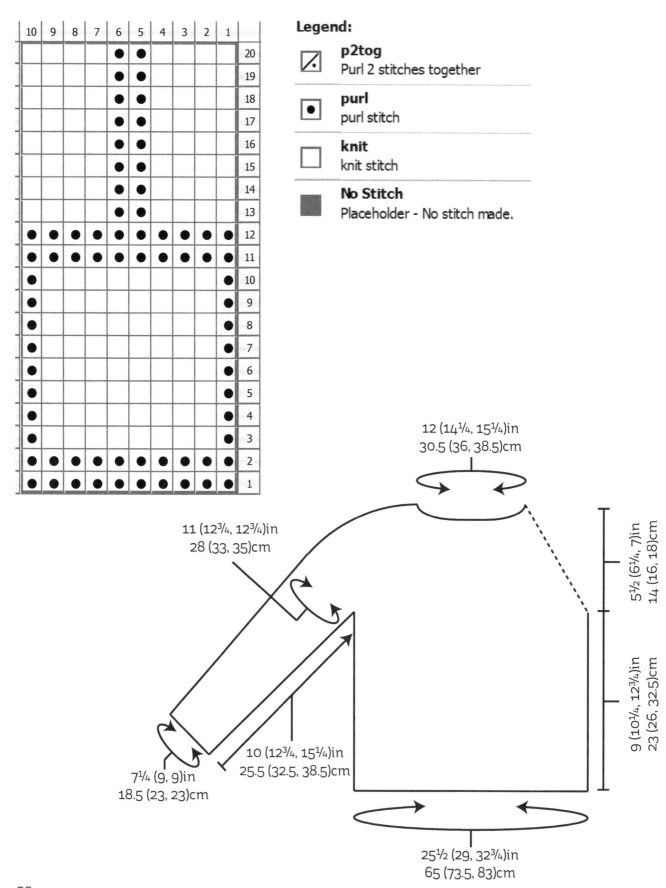

Legend:

- **p2tog** — Purl 2 stitches together
- **purl** — purl stitch
- **knit** — knit stitch
- **No Stitch** — Placeholder - No stitch made.

12 (14¼, 15¼)in
30.5 (36, 38.5)cm

11 (12¾, 12¾)in
28 (33, 35)cm

5½ (6¼, 7)in
14 (16, 18)cm

10 (12¾, 15¼)in
25.5 (32.5, 38.5)cm

7¼ (9, 9)in
18.5 (23, 23)cm

9 (10¼, 12¾)in
23 (26, 32.5)cm

25½ (29, 32¾)in
65 (73.5, 83)cm

Yoke Chart: Size 4

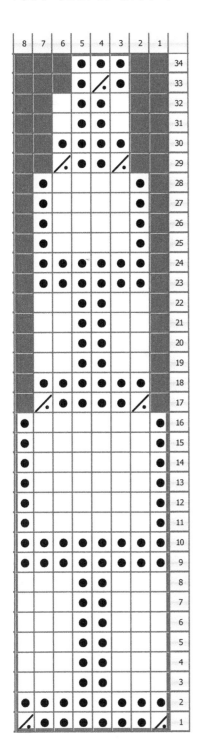

Yoke Chart: Size 6-8

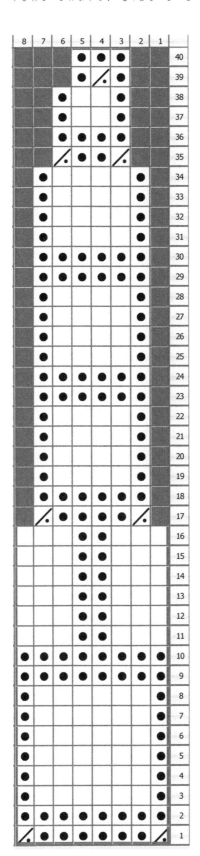

Yoke Chart: Size 10-12

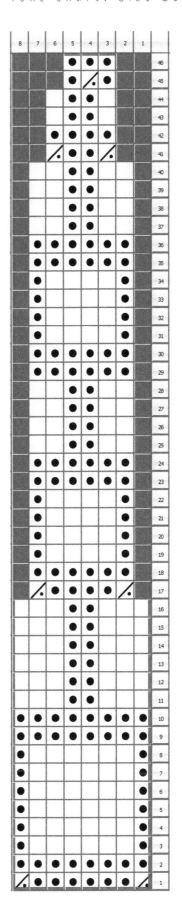

SPACER

This asymmetrical sweater is knit in the round from the bottom up. Set-in sleeves are joined with the body at the armhole and then worked together to the collar.

SIZE & SKILL LEVEL

Finished chest circ - 25¾ (27½, 29¼, 31, 32¾, 34¾)in / 65 (70, 74.5, 78.5, 83, 88.5)cm. To fit sizes 4 (6, 8, 10, 12, 14). Shown in size 10.
Intermediate difficulty - Knit, purl, cabling, decreases, picking up stitches, working in the round, short rows.

MATERIALS AND NOTIONS

6 (6, 6, 7, 7, 8) balls of Debbie Bliss Rialto Aran (100% wool; 50g / 81 yds / 75m); #11 teal blue.
US7 (4.5mm) and US8 (5mm) double-pointed and circular needles (24in / 60cm long). Adjust needle size as needed to obtain correct gauge.
Stitch markers, cable needle (cn), stitch holders, and tapestry needle.

GAUGE

18 sts and 24 rows = 4in / 10cm in St st using larger needles.

STITCH PATTERNS

2x2 Rib (multiple of 4 sts)
Rnd 1: *K2, p2; rep from * to end.
Rep Rnd 1 for patt.

(Charts begin on page 73.)

BODY

With smaller circular needle, CO 116 (124, 132, 140, 148, 156) sts, pm and join to work in the round. Work in 2x2 Rib for 1½in / 4cm. Change to larger needle. Inc rnd: *K29 (31, 33, 35, 37, 39), pm, [k2, m1] 12 (12, 16, 16, 16, 16) times, pm, knit to end.

Work appropriate size body chart between markers and all other sts in St st through last rnd of chart. Remove chart markers. 116 (124, 132, 140, 148, 156) sts. On next rnd, place a side seam marker after 58 (62, 66, 70, 74, 78) sts.

Work even in St st until body measures 9½ (10, 11, 12, 13, 13½)in / 24 (25.5, 28, 30.5, 33, 34.5)cm from cast-on edge.
Next rnd: Knit to 2 (3, 3, 3, 3, 3) sts past side seam marker, place 4 (6, 6, 6, 6, 6) sts just worked on a holder, knit to 2 (3, 3, 3, 3, 3) sts past beg-of-rnd marker, place 4 (6, 6, 6, 6, 6) sts just worked on a holder. 54 (56, 60, 64, 68, 72) sts rem for each half of body. Leave sts on circular needle with yarn attached.

LEFT SLEEVE

With smaller dpns, CO 32 (36, 36, 40, 40, 40) sts, pm and join to work in the round. Work in 2x2 Rib for 1½in / 4cm.
Change to larger needles and St st. Knit 1 rnd. Inc 1 st at the beg and end of next rnd, then every foll 8th rnd 6 (5, 6, 6, 8, 10) times more. 46 (48, 50, 54, 58, 62) sts.
Work even until sleeve measures 10½ (12, 13½, 14¼, 15½, 17½)in / 26.5 (30.5, 34.5, 36, 42, 44.5)cm from cast-on edge, ending last rnd 2 (3, 3, 3, 3, 3) sts before the marker. Place next 4 (6, 6, 6, 6, 6) sts on a holder. 42 (42, 44, 48, 52, 56) sts.

RIGHT SLEEVE

With smaller dpns, CO 32 (36, 36, 40, 40, 40) sts, pm and join to work in the round.
Work in 2x2 Rib for 1½in / 4cm. Change to larger needles. Inc rnd: K12 (14, 14, 16, 16, 16), pm, [k2, m1] 4 times, pm, knit to end.
Work sleeve chart between markers and all other sts in St st. Work Rnds 1-8 of chart 6 (7, 8, 8, 9, 11) times, then Rnds 9-14 once; remove chart markers.
AT THE SAME TIME, inc 1 st at the beg and end of next rnd, then every foll 8th rnd 6 (5, 6, 6, 8, 10) times more. 46 (48, 50, 54, 58, 62) sts. Work even until sleeve measures 10½ (12, 13½, 14¼, 15½, 17½)in / 26.5 (30.5, 34.5, 36, 42, 44.5)cm from cast-on edge, ending last rnd 2 (3, 3, 3, 3, 3) sts before the marker. Place next 4 (6, 6, 6, 6, 6) sts on a holder. 42 (42, 44, 48, 52, 56) sts.

YOKE

Join sleeves and body: Knit across 54 (56, 60, 64, 68, 72) front sts, pm, k42 (42, 44, 48, 52, 56) right sleeve sts, pm, k54 (56, 60, 64, 68, 72) back sts, pm, k42 (42, 44, 48, 52, 56) left sleeve sts, pm. 192 (196, 208, 224, 240, 256) sts.

Shape armholes:
Dec rnd 1: *Ssk, work to 2 sts before marker, k2tog, sm; rep from * 3 times more. (8 sts dec'd.)
Rep Dec rnd 1 on every 2nd rnd twice more. 48 (50, 54, 58, 62, 66) sts each on front and back, 36 (36, 38, 42, 46, 50) sts each sleeve.

Shape sleeve caps:
Work 2 rnds even.
Dec rnd 2: *Knit to marker, sm, ssk, work to 2 sts before next marker, k2tog, sm; rep from * once more. (4 sts dec'd.)
Rep Dec rnd 2 on every 3rd rnd 1 (4, 5, 5, 4, 3) times more, then on every 2nd rnd 5 (2, 2, 4, 7, 10) times, then on every rnd 2 times. 18 sts rem in each sleeve.

Shape sleeve caps and front neck:
Row 1 (RS): *Knit to marker, sm, ssk, turn.
Row 2 (WS): Sl1, sm, purl to marker, sm, p2tog, turn.
Row 3: Sl1, sm, knit to marker, sm, ssk, turn.
Row 4: Rep Row 2.
Row 5: Sl1, sm, k20 (20, 21, 23, 24, 26), BO center 8 (10, 12, 12, 14, 14) sts, knit to marker, sm, ssk, turn.

Right front shoulder:
Row 1 (WS): Sl1, sm, purl to end.
Row 2 (RS): BO 2 sts, knit to marker, sm, ssk, turn.
Rows 3-6: Rep Rows 1-2.
Row 7: Sl1, sm, purl to end.
Row 8: BO 1 st, knit to marker, sm, ssk, turn.
Rows 9-10: Rep Rows 7-8. Place these 13 (13, 14, 16, 17, 19) sts on a holder.

Left front shoulder:
Join yarn at neck edge with WS facing.
Row 1 (WS): BO 2 sts, purl to marker, sm, p2tog, turn.
Row 2 (RS): Sl1, sm, knit to end.
Rows 3-6: Rep Rows 1-2.
Row 7: BO 1 st, purl to marker, sm, p2tog, turn.
Row 8: Sl1, sm, knit to end.
Rows 9-10: Rep Rows 7-8.
Row 11: Purl to marker, sm, p2tog, turn. Place these 13 (13, 14, 16, 17, 19) sts on a holder.

Shape back shoulders:
Join yarn with RS facing, 1 st before the right back sleeve marker.
Row 1 (RS): Sl1, sm, knit to marker, sm, ssk, turn.
Row 2 (WS): Sl1, sm, purl to marker, sm, p2tog, turn.
Rep Rows 1-2 7 times more. 50 (52, 56, 60, 64, 68) sts.
Leave sts on needle with yarn attached.

FINISHING

With right sides facing, join right shoulder using a 3-needle bind off, BO next 24 (26, 28, 28, 30, 30) sts for back neck, join left shoulder using a 3-needle bind off.

Collar
With smaller dpns, pick up and knit 1 st in every st and 3 sts for every 4 rows around neck, pm.
Count sts and adjust to a multiple of 4 on next rnd, if needed. Work 2x2 Rib for 1in / 2.5cm. BO in patt.

Graft underarms. Weave in ends and block according to ball band instructions if desired.

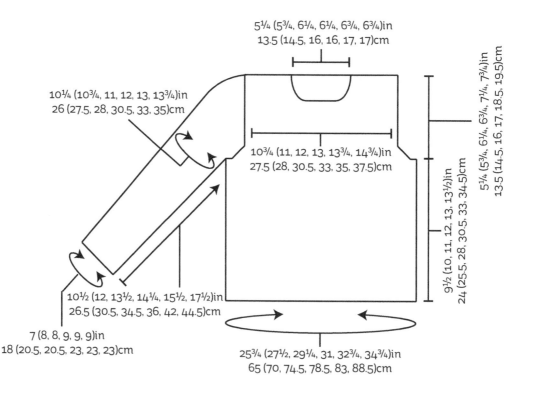

5¼ (5¾, 6¼, 6¼, 6¾, 6¾)in
13.5 (14.5, 16, 16, 17, 17)cm

10¼ (10¾, 11, 12, 13, 13¾)in
26 (27.5, 28, 30.5, 33, 35)cm

10¾ (11, 12, 13, 13¾, 14¾)in
27.5 (28, 30.5, 33, 35, 37.5)cm

5¼ (5¾, 6¼, 6¾, 7¼, 7¾)in
13.5 (14.5, 16, 17, 18.5, 19.5)cm

9½ (10, 11, 12, 13, 13½)in
24 (25.5, 28, 30.5, 33, 34.5)cm

10½ (12, 13½, 14¼, 15½, 17½)in
26.5 (30.5, 34.5, 36, 42, 44.5)cm

7 (8, 8, 9, 9, 9)in
18 (20.5, 20.5, 23, 23, 23)cm

25¾ (27½, 29¼, 31, 32¾, 34¾)in
65 (70, 74.5, 78.5, 83, 88.5)cm

Body Chart: Sizes 4 & 6

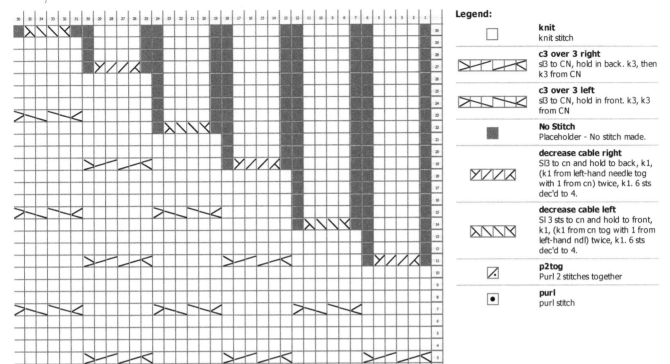

Legend:

☐	**knit**	knit stitch
⬡	**c3 over 3 right**	sl3 to CN, hold in back. k3, then k3 from CN
⬡	**c3 over 3 left**	sl3 to CN, hold in front. k3, k3 from CN
⬛	**No Stitch**	Placeholder - No stitch made.
⬡	**decrease cable right**	Sl3 to cn and hold to back, k1, (k1 from left-hand needle tog with 1 from cn) twice, k1. 6 sts dec'd to 4.
⬡	**decrease cable left**	Sl 3 sts to cn and hold to front, k1, (k1 from cn tog with 1 from left-hand ndl) twice, k1. 6 sts dec'd to 4.
◿	**p2tog**	Purl 2 stitches together
⊙	**purl**	purl stitch

Body Chart: Sizes 8 & 10

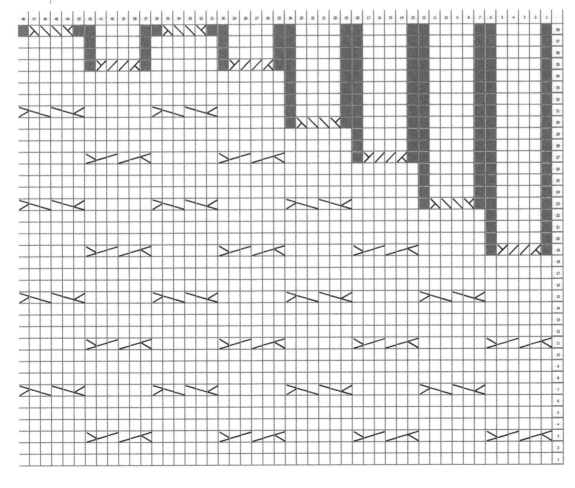

73

Body Chart: Sizes 12 & 14

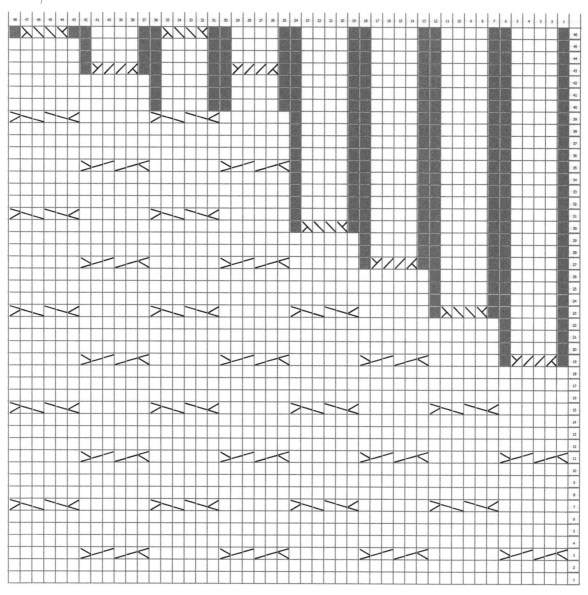

Legend:

☐	knit
c3 over 3 right	c3 over 3 right
c3 over 3 left	c3 over 3 left
■	No Stitch
decrease cable right	decrease cable right
decrease cable left	decrease cable left

Sleeve Chart: All Sizes

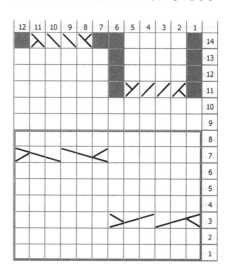

TARADIDDLE

As the name of this sweater suggests, the colorwork is not what it may seem at a first glance. Mosaic stitch is essentially a slip-stitch knitting that looks like stranded knitting – but is easier to execute, since only one color is used in any given round. The mock V-neck is knitted in the same stripe sequence as the body and therefore is worked simultaneously with it. Slipped stitches on either side of the V help to embed the simple stripe into the patterned body and bring the two together.

SIZE & SKILL LEVEL

Finished chest circ - 26 (27½, 29, 30½, 32, 33½)in / 66 (70, 73.5, 77.5, 81.5, 85)cm. To fit sizes 4 (6, 8, 10, 12, 14). Shown in size 10.
Intermediate difficulty - Knit, purl, decreases, slipped sts, picking up sts, working in the round, short rows.

MATERIALS AND NOTIONS

3 (4, 4, 4, 4, 4) balls of Alba DK (100% wool; 50g / 131 yds / 120m); Navy (MC).
3 (3, 3, 3, 4, 4) balls of Jamieson & Smith Shetland DK (100% undyed Shetland wool; 50g /188yds / 172m); #2002 Mooskit (CC).
US4 (3.5mm) and US6 (4mm) double-pointed and circular needles (24in / 60cm long). Adjust needle size as needed to obtain correct gauge.
Stitch markers in two colors, stitch holders, row counter, and tapestry needle.

GAUGE

21 sts and 29 rnds = 4in / 10cm in Mosaic Pattern using larger needles.

STITCH PATTERNS

2x2 Rib (multiple of 4 sts)
Rnd 1: *K2, p2; rep from * to end.
Rep Rnd 1.

Stripe Pattern for sleeves and neck inset
Work in St st: 2 rows/rnds MC, 2 rows/rnds CC. For neck inset, use same color as for current rnd of Mosaic Pattern on body.

(See next page for Mosaic Pattern chart.)

BODY

With MC and smaller circular needle, CO 136 (144, 152, 160, 168, 176) sts, pm color A and join to work in the rnd.
Work in 2x2 Rib for 1½in / 4cm. On last rnd, place a second A marker after 68 (72, 76, 80, 84, 88) sts.

Change to larger needle and work in Mosaic Pattern until piece measures 9 (10, 11, 12, 13, 13½)in / 23 (25.5, 28, 30.5, 33, 34.5)cm from cast on, ending with an even-numbered rnd of patt. Next rnd: Work in patt to 3 sts past first marker, place last 6 sts (3 sts either side of underarm marker) on a holder, work to last 3 sts, place next 6 sts (3 sts either side of beg-of-rnd marker) on a holder. Do not break yarn.

SLEEVES

With MC and smaller dpns, CO 40 (40, 44, 44, 48, 48) sts, pm color A and join to work in the rnd. Work in 2x2 Rib for 1½in / 4cm. Change to larger needles and Stripe Pattern. Inc 1 st at beg and end of next rnd, then every foll 10th rnd 5 (7, 7, 9, 9, 11) more times. 52 (56, 60, 64, 68, 72) sts.
Work even until sleeve measures 10½ (11¾, 13, 14¼, 15½, 17)in / 26.5 (30, 33, 36, 39.5, 43)cm from cast on, ending with the same color stripe as the last rnd on the body. Stop working last rnd 3 sts before the marker. Place next 6 sts on a holder for underarm. 46 (50, 54, 58, 62, 66) sts. Break yarn leaving a long tail for grafting underarms.

YOKE

Join sleeves and body: Arrange sts on larger circular needle in the foll order: 46 (50, 54, 58, 62, 66) sts of left sleeve, pm color A, 30 (32, 34, 36, 38, 40) front sts, pm color B, 2 front sts, pm color B, 30 (32, 34, 36, 38, 40) front sts, pm color A, 46 (50, 54, 58, 62, 66) sts of right sleeve, pm color A, 62 (66, 70, 74, 78, 82) back sts, pm color A. Rnd begins just before left sleeve, using yarn still attached to body. 216 (232, 248, 264, 280, 296) sts.

Set your row counter to zero. Cont working body in Main stitch patt and sleeves in Stripe patt throughout yoke. PLEASE READ AHEAD: yoke shaping and neck inset will be worked simultaneously.

Shape yoke:
Dec rnd 1: *Work to A marker, sm, ssk, work to 2 sts before next A marker, k2tog, sm; rep from * once more. (4 sts dec'd.)
Rep Dec Rnd 1 twice more. 56 (60, 64, 68, 72, 76) sts each on back and front, 46 (50, 54, 58, 62, 66) sts each sleeve.
Work 1 rnd even.
Dec rnd 2: *Ssk, work to 2 sts before A marker, k2tog, sm, work to next A marker, sm; rep from * once more. (4 sts dec'd.)
Rep Dec Rnd 2 on every other rnd 2 (4, 5, 5, 6, 8) times more, then on every rnd 12 (12, 12, 14, 14, 14) times. 56 (60, 64, 68, 72, 76) sts each on back and front; 16 (16, 18, 18, 20, 20) sts each sleeve.

AT THE SAME TIME, beg on 8th (10th, 12th, 14th, 16th, 18th) rnd of yoke, begin shaping front neck inset as foll:
Mock V-neck is achieved by decreasing on the outside of the center front (B) markers, while increasing inside the B markers so the overall stitch count remains constant. Stitches between the B markers are worked in Stripe Pattern.
Rnd 1: Work as set to 2 sts before 1st B marker, k2tog, sm, m1L, knit to next B marker, m1R, sm, ssk, work as set to end of rnd.
Rnd 2: Work as set to 1 st before 1st B marker, sl1, sm, knit to next B marker, sm, sl1, work as set to end of rnd.
Rep Rnds 1-2 through end of neck shaping.

Shape back shoulders and sleeve caps:
Sm, k1, turn.
Row 1 (WS): Sl1, sm, work in patt to A marker, sm, p2tog, turn.
Row 2 (RS): Sl1, sm, work in patt to A marker, sm, ssk, turn.
Rep Rows 1-2 6 (6, 7, 7, 8, 8) times more. 58 (62, 66, 70, 74, 78) sts. Place sts on holder.

Shape left front shoulder, neck, and sleeve cap:
Join yarn 1 st before left front A marker with RS facing.
Sl1, sm, work 23 (25, 26, 28, 29, 31) sts in patt, turn.
Row 1 (WS): BO 3 sts, work to A marker, sm, p2tog, turn.
Row 2: Sl1, sm, work to end.
Row 3: BO 2 sts, work to A marker, sm, p2tog, turn.
Row 4: Rep Row 2.
Row 5: BO 1 st, work to A marker, sm, p2tog, turn.
Row 6: Rep Row 2.
Rep Rows 5-6 3 (3, 4, 4, 4, 4) times more.
Next row (WS): Work to A marker, sm, p2tog, turn.
Next row (RS): Sl1, sm, work to end.
Rep the last 2 rows 0 (0, 0, 0, 1, 1) time(s) more. 15 (17, 17, 19, 20, 22) sts. Place sts on holder.

Shape right front shoulder, neck, and sleeve cap:
Join yarn at neck edge on RS, BO 10 (10, 12, 12, 14, 14) sts, work to A marker, sm, ssk, turn.

Row 1 (WS): Sl1, sm, work to end.
Row 2 (RS): BO 3 sts, work to A marker, sm, ssk, turn.
Row 3: Rep Row 1.
Row 4: BO 2 sts, work to A marker, sm, ssk, turn.
Row 5: Rep Row 1.
Row 6: BO 1 st, work to A marker, sm, ssk, turn.
Rep Rows 5-6 3 (3, 4, 4, 4, 4) times more.

SIZES 12 AND 14 ONLY:
Next row (WS): Sl1, sm, work to end.
Next row (RS): Work to A marker, sm, ssk.

ALL SIZES:
15 (17, 17, 19, 20, 22) sts. Place sts on holder.

FINISHING
With right sides facing, join right shoulder using a 3-needle bind off, BO next 28 (28, 32, 32, 34, 34) sts for back neck, join left shoulder using a 3-needle bind off.

Collar
Using smaller needles, with MC and RS facing and starting at one of the shoulder seams, pick up and knit 1 st in each bound-off st around neck. Work in St st for 1 in / 2.5 cm. BO loosely.

Graft underarms, weave in ends and block if desired according to the ball band instructions.

Mosaic Pattern Chart

knit
knit stitch

slip
Slip stitch as if to purl, holding yarn in back

(Multiple of 8 sts.)
Rnds 1-2: With MC, knit.
Rnds 3-4: With CC *Sl1, k6, sl1; rep from * to end.
Rnds 5-6: With MC, knit.
Rnds 7-8: With CC, *K3, sl2, k3; rep from * to end.
Rep Rnds 1-8.

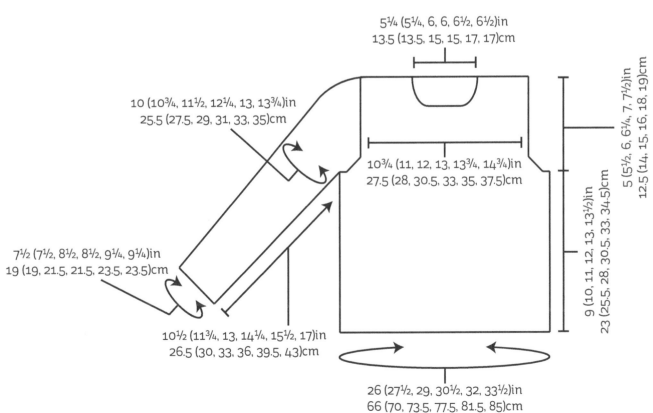

5¼ (5¼, 6, 6, 6½, 6½)in
13.5 (13.5, 15, 15, 17, 17)cm

5 (5½, 6, 6¼, 7, 7½)in
12.5 (14, 15, 16, 18, 19)cm

10 (10¾, 11½, 12¼, 13, 13¾)in
25.5 (27.5, 29, 31, 33, 35)cm

10¾ (11, 12, 13, 13¾, 14¾)in
27.5 (28, 30.5, 33, 35, 37.5)cm

9 (10, 11, 12, 13, 13½)in
23 (25.5, 28, 30.5, 33, 34.5)cm

7½ (7½, 8½, 8½, 9¼, 9¼)in
19 (19, 21.5, 21.5, 23.5, 23.5)cm

10½ (11¾, 13, 14¼, 15½, 17)in
26.5 (30, 33, 36, 39.5, 43)cm

26 (27½, 29, 30½, 32, 33½)in
66 (70, 73.5, 77.5, 81.5, 85)cm

BUSTER

This cardigan is knit seamlessly from the bottom up. Set-in sleeves are joined with the body at the armhole and then worked together to the collar. Its rich texture is achieved by cabling knit and purl stitches that are set on the purl ground.

SIZE & SKILL LEVEL

Finished chest circ - 26½ (29¼, 32, 34¾, 37¼)in / 67.5 (74.5, 81.5, 88.5, 94.5)cm, zipped. To fit sizes 4 (6-8, 10, 12, 14). Shown in size 12.
Intermediate difficulty - Knit, purl, cabling, decreases, picking up stitches, working in the round, short rows.

MATERIALS AND NOTIONS

6 (7, 7, 8, 9) skeins of Artesano Aran Alpaca Blend (50% alpaca, 50% wool; 100g / 144yds / 132m); #2200 Laxford.
US6 (4mm) and US8 (5mm) double-pointed and circular needles (24in / 60cm long). Adjust needle size as needed to obtain correct gauge.
Approx. 15½ (17½, 19¼, 20½, 21)in / 39 (44, 49, 52.5, 53) cm separating zipper.
Stitch markers, cable needle (cn), tapestry needle, sewing needle and thread.

GAUGE

24 sts and 24 rows = 4in / 10cm in Cable patt using larger needles.

STITCH PATTERNS

Ribbing (multiple of 12 sts)
Row 1 (RS): *P1, k3, p4, k3, p1; rep from * to end.
Row 2: *K1, p3, k4, p3, k1; rep from * to end.
Rep Rows 1-2 for patt.

2x2 Rib (multiple of 4 sts + 2)
Row 1 (WS): *P2, k2; rep from * to last 2 sts, p2.
Row 2: *K2, p2; rep from * to last 2 sts, k2.
Rep Rows 1-2 for patt.

(See page 83 for Cable Pattern chart.)

SLEEVES

With smaller dpns, CO 32 (36, 36, 40, 40) sts, pm and join for working in the rnd.
Set up rib rnd: K3 (0, 0, 1, 1), p1 (0, 0, 1, 1), [p1, k3, p4, k3, p1] 2 (3, 3, 3, 3) times, p1 (0, 0, 1, 1), k3 (0, 0, 1, 1).
Rep last rnd for 2in / 5cm.
Inc rnd: K3 (0, 0, 1, 1), p1 (0, 0, 1, 1), pm, [p1, k3, (pfb) 4 times, k3, p1] 2 (3, 3, 3, 3) times, pm, p1 (0, 0, 1, 1), k3 (0, 0, 1, 1). 40 (48, 48, 52, 52) sts. Change to larger needles.

Set up sleeve patt: K3 (0, 0, 1, 1), p1 (0, 0, 1, 1), sm, work cable patt to next marker, sm, p1 (0, 0, 1, 1), k3 (0, 0, 1, 1). Cont in est patt, inc 1 st at beg and end of next rnd, then every foll 4th (6th, 6th, 6th, 6th) rnd 10 (8, 10, 10, 12) more times. 62 (66, 70, 74, 78) sts. Work increased stitches into the patt as far as possible. When the number of sts between beg-of-rnd marker and markers surrounding patt repeats allow for half a patt repeat to be worked, shift markers around patt repeats toward beg-of-rnd marker.

Work even until sleeve measures 10½ (13½, 15, 16, 17½) in / 26.5 (34.5, 38, 40.5, 44.5)cm or desired length from cast-on edge, ending with an even-numbered rnd, and stopping last rnd 4 sts before the beg-of-rnd marker. Make a note of the last rnd of the cable patt worked. Place 4 sts on either side of beg of rnd marker onto a holder. 54 (58, 62, 66, 70) sts.

BODY

With smaller circular needle, CO 120 (132, 144, 156, 168) sts. Do not join. Work in Ribbing for 2 (2, 1½, 1½, 2)in / 5 (5, 4, 4, 5)cm, ending with a RS row. Note: For a clean front edge, slip the first stitch of each row instead of knitting or purling it. Change to larger needle. Inc row (WS): *K1, p3, [kfb] 4 times, p3, k1; rep from * to end. 160 (176, 192, 208, 224) sts. Change to Cable patt and work even until body measures 9 (11, 12½, 13½, 13½)in / 23 (28, 32, 34.5, 34.5)cm from cast-on edge, ending with the same patt row as on the sleeves.

YOKE

Next row (RS): Work 36 (40, 44, 48, 52) right front sts, place next 8 sts on holder for underarm, pm, work 54 (58, 62, 66, 70) sleeve sts, pm, work 72 (80, 88, 96, 104) back sts, place next 8 sts on holder for underarm, pm, work 54 (58, 62, 66, 70) sleeve sts, pm, work 36 (40, 44, 48, 52) left front sts. 252 (276, 300, 324, 348) sts. Work 1 WS row even.

Shape armholes:
Dec row 1 (RS): *Work to 2 sts before marker, k2tog, sm, ssk; rep from * 3 more times, work to end. (8 sts dec'd.)
Dec row 2 (WS): *Work to 2 sts before marker, p2tog tbl, sm, p2tog; rep from * 3 more times, work to end. (8 sts dec'd.)
Rep Dec Rows 1-2 1 (1, 1, 2, 3) more times. 32 (36, 40, 42, 44) front sts; 46 (50, 54, 54, 54) sleeve sts; 64 (72, 80, 84, 88) back sts.

Shape sleeve caps:
Dec row 3 (RS): *Work to marker, sm, ssk, work to 2 sts before marker, k2tog, sm; rep from * once more, work to end. (4 sts dec'd on sleeves only.)
Dec row 4 (WS): *Work to marker, sm, p2tog, work to 2 sts before marker, p2tog tbl, sm; rep from * once more, work to end. (4 sts dec'd on sleeves only.)
Rep Dec Rows 3-4 5 (6, 7, 6, 6) more times, then Dec Row 3 1 (0, 0, 1, 1) time more. 20 (22, 22, 24, 24) rem in each sleeve. Work 1 (0, 0, 1, 1) row even.

Right front sleeve cap and neck shaping:
Row 1 (RS): Work to marker, sm, ssk, turn.
Row 2 (WS): Sl1, sm, work to end.
Rows 3-10: Rep Rows 1-2.
Row 11 (RS): BO 12 (13, 14, 15, 16) sts, work to marker, sm, ssk. 20 (23, 26, 27, 28) front sts rem.
Row 12: Sl1, sm, work to last 2 sts, p2tog tbl. (1 st dec'd at neck.)
Row 13: Ssk, work to marker, sm, ssk, turn. (1 st dec'd at neck.)
Row 14: Rep Row 12.
Row 15: Sl1, sm, work to end.
Row 16: Rep Row 12. 16 (19, 22, 23, 24) front sts rem.
Row 17: Work to marker, sm, ssk, turn.
Row 18: Sl1, sm, work to end.
Rep Rows 17-18 another 0 (1, 1, 2, 2) times. 17 (20, 23, 24, 25) sts rem for shoulder.

Left front sleeve cap and neck shaping:
Join yarn at front edge with WS facing.
Row 1 (WS): Work to marker, sm, p2tog, turn.
Row 2: Sl1, sm, work to end.
Rows 3-10: Rep Rows 1-2.
Row 11 (WS): BO 12 (13, 14, 15, 16) sts, work to marker, sm, p2tog. 20 (23, 26, 27, 28) front sts rem.
Row 12: Sl1, sm, work to last 2 sts, k2tog. (1 st dec'd at neck.)
Row 13: P2tog, work to marker, sm, p2tog, turn. (1 st dec'd at neck.)
Row 14: Rep Row 12.

Row 15: Work to marker, sm, p2tog, turn.
Row 16: Rep Row 12. 16 (19, 22, 23, 24) front sts rem.
Row 17: Work to marker, sm, p2tog, turn.
Row 18: Sl1, sm, work to end.
Rep Rows 17-18 another 0 (1, 1, 2, 2) times. 17 (20, 23, 24, 25) sts rem for shoulder. Place sts on holder.

Back sleeve cap and neck shaping:
With RS facing, join yarn 1 st before the back right sleeve marker.
Row 1 (RS): Sl1, sm, work to marker, sm, ssk, turn.
Row 2: Sl1, sm, work to marker, sm, p2tog, turn.
Rep last 2 rows 7 (8, 8, 9, 9) more times.
Right shoulder:
Next row (RS): Sl1, sm, work 19 (22, 25, 26, 27) in patt, turn.
Next row (WS): BO 3 sts, work to marker, sm, p2tog, turn.
Next row: Sl1, sm, work to end. 17 (20, 23, 24, 25) sts rem for shoulder. Place sts on holder.
Left shoulder:
With RS facing, join yarn to remaining sts and BO 26 (28, 30, 32, 34) sts, work to marker, sm, ssk, turn. 19 (22, 25, 26, 27) back sts rem.
Next row (WS): Sl1, sm, work to end.
Next row: BO 3 sts, work to marker, sm, ssk. 17 (20, 23, 24, 25) sts rem for shoulder. Place sts on holder.

FINISHING
Join shoulders using a 3-needle bind off.

Collar
With smaller needles and RS facing, pick up and knit 1 st in every bound-off st and 1 st in every row around right front neck, back neck and left front neck. Adjust if needed to achieve a multiple of 4 sts + 2.
Work in 2x2 Rib until collar measures 3½in / 9cm. BO in patt.

Graft underarms, weave in ends and block if desired according to ball band instructions. Pin the zipper in place, starting from the hem and working up to 1¾in / 4cm past the beginning of the collar. Fold collar in half inward, covering the top end of the zipper but leaving the teeth out. Sew zipper and collar in place.

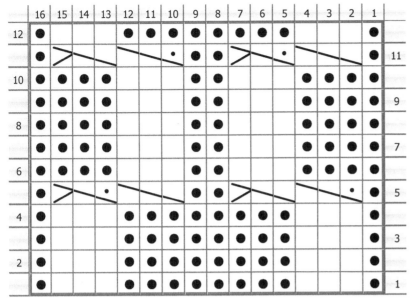

Legend:

	purl
[•]	RS: purl stitch WS: knit stitch

	knit
[ ]	RS: knit stitch WS: purl stitch

	c3 over 3 left P
	RS: sl3 to CN, hold in front. p3, k3 from CN WS: none defined

	c3 purled over 3 left
	RS: Sl3 to CN and hold to front, k3, p3 from CN. WS:

Cable Pattern
(Multiple of 16 sts.)

Rows/rnds 1 & 3: *P1, k3, p8, k3, p1; rep from * to end.

Row/rnd 2 (and every WS row/alternate rnd): Work each stitch as it presents itself (knit the knits and purl the purls).

Row/rnd 5: *P1, sl 3 to cn and hold to front, p3, k3 from cn, p2, sl 3 to cn and hold to front, k3, p3 from cn, p1; rep from * to end.

Rows/rnds 7 & 9: *P4, k3, p2, k3, p4; rep from * to end.

Row/rnd 11: *P1, sl 3 to cn and hold to front, k3, p3 from cn, p2, sl 3 to cn and hold to front, p3, k3 from cn, p1; rep from * to end.

Row/rnd 12: Work each stitch as it presents itself.

Rep Rows/Rnds 1-12 for patt.

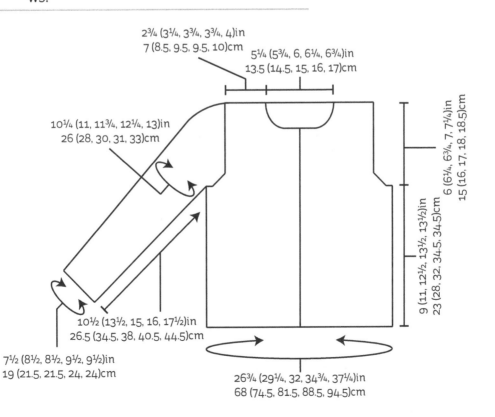

2¾ (3¼, 3¾, 3¾, 4)in
7 (8.5, 9.5, 9.5, 10)cm

5¼ (5¾, 6, 6¼, 6¾)in
13.5 (14.5, 15, 16, 17)cm

10¼ (11, 11¾, 12¼, 13)in
26 (28, 30, 31, 33)cm

6 (6¼, 6¾, 7, 7¼)in
15 (16, 17, 18, 18.5)cm

9 (11, 12½, 13½, 13½)in
23 (28, 32, 34.5, 34.5)cm

10½ (13½, 15, 16, 17½)in
26.5 (34.5, 38, 40.5, 44.5)cm

7½ (8½, 8½, 9½, 9½)in
19 (21.5, 21.5, 24, 24)cm

26¾ (29¼, 32, 34¾, 37¼)in
68 (74.5, 81.5, 88.5, 94.5)cm

83

CHIP

Chip is knit seamlessly from the bottom up with set in sleeves and a fold over collar. A good balance of stockinette and slinky ribbing make this a very wearable wardrobe staple.

SIZE & SKILL LEVEL

Finished chest circ - 27¼ (28¾, 30½, 32, 33½, 36¾)in / 69 (73, 77.5, 81.5, 85, 93.5)cm. To fit sizes 4 (6, 8, 10, 12, 14). Shown in size 10.
Intermediate difficulty - Knit, purl, decreases, picking up stitches, working in the round, short rows.

MATERIALS AND NOTIONS

4 (4, 4, 4, 5, 5) skeins of Cascade Yarns 220 Superwash (100% superwash wool; 100g / 220yds / 201m); #891 green.
US6 (4mm) and US7 (4.5mm) double-pointed and circular needles (32in / 80cm long). Adjust needle size as needed to obtain correct gauge.
Approx. 15¼ (16¼, 17½, 18¾, 20½, 21¼)in / 38.5 (41.5, 44.5, 47.5, 52, 54)cm separating zipper.
Stitch markers in two colors, tapestry needle, stitch holders, sewing needle and thread.

GAUGE

20 sts and 28 rows = 4in / 10cm in St st using larger needles.

STITCH PATTERNS

2x2 Rib worked flat (multiple of 4 sts)
Row 1 (RS): *K1, p2, k1; rep from * to end.
Row 2 (WS): *P1, k2, p1; rep from * to end.
Rep Rows 1-2.

2x2 Rib worked in the round (multiple of 4 sts)
Rnd 1: *K1, p2, k1; rep from * to end.
Rep Rnd 1.

BODY

With smaller circular needle, CO 136 (144, 152, 160, 168, 184) sts. Work in 2x2 Rib for 1¼in / 3cm, ending with a WS row. Change to larger needle.

Set up patt (RS): Work 11 sts in est rib, pm color A, k18 (18, 22, 22, 22, 26), pm color A, work 10 (14, 10, 14, 18, 18) sts in est rib, pm color A, k58 (58, 66, 66, 66, 74), pm color A, work 10 (14, 10, 14, 18, 18) sts in est rib, pm color A, k18 (18, 22, 22, 22, 26), pm color A, work 11 sts in rib.
Next row (WS): Work 11 sts rib, sm, *purl to marker, sm, work rib to marker, sm; rep from * once more, purl to last marker, sm, work rib to end.
Cont in St st with rib panels until body measures 9 (10, 11, 12, 13, 13.5)in / 23 (25.5, 28, 30.5, 33, 34.5)cm from cast on, ending with a WS row. Do not break yarn.

SLEEVES

With smaller dpns, CO 36 (36, 36, 44, 44, 44) sts, pm color B and join for working in the rnd.
Work in 2x2 Rib for 1¼in / 3cm, ending with a WS row.

Change to larger needles.
Set up patt: K13 (13, 13, 17, 17, 17), pm color A, work 10 sts in est rib patt, pm color A, k13 (13, 13, 17, 17, 17).
Next rnd: Knit to marker increasing 3 (4, 4, 2, 3, 4) sts evenly spaced, sm, rib to next marker, sm, knit to end increasing 3 (4, 4, 2, 3, 4) sts evenly spaced. 42 (44, 44, 48, 50, 52) sts.

Cont in St st with rib panel, inc 1 st at beg and end of next rnd, then every foll 9th (10th, 9th, 10th, 12th, 12th) rnd 6 (6, 8, 7, 7, 7) times more. 56 (58, 62, 64, 66, 68) sts. Work even until sleeve measures 10½ (11¾, 13, 14¼, 15½, 17)in / 26.5 (30, 33, 36, 39.5, 43)cm from cast on, ending last rnd 2 (2, 3, 3, 4, 4) sts before the B marker. Place next 4 (4, 6, 6, 8, 8) sts on a holder. 52 (54, 56, 58, 58, 60) sts. Break yarn leaving a long tail for grafting underarm.

YOKE

Join sleeves and body: With RS facing and circular ndl, maintaining est st patterns on body and sleeves, work 32 (34, 35, 37, 38, 42) right front sts, place next 4 (4, 6, 6, 8, 8) sts on a holder, pm color B, work across 52 (54, 56, 58, 58, 60) sleeve sts, pm color B, work 64 (68, 70, 74, 76, 84) back sts, place next 4 (4, 6, 6, 8, 8) sts on a holder, pm color B, work across 52 (54, 56, 58, 58, 60) sleeve sts, pm color B, work 32 (34, 35, 37, 38, 42) left front sts. 232 (244, 252, 264, 268, 288) sts total.

Work 1 WS row even.

Shape armholes:
Dec row 1 (RS): *Work to 2 sts before B marker, k2tog, sm, work to next B marker, sm, ssk; rep from * once more, work to end. (4 sts dec'd.)
Dec row 2 (WS): *Work to 2 sts before B marker, ssp, sm, work to next B marker, sm, p2tog; rep from * once more, work to end. (4 sts dec'd.)
Rep Dec Rows 1-2 twice more. 26 (28, 29, 31, 32, 36) sts rem each front, 52 (56, 58, 62, 64, 72) back sts, 52 (54, 56, 58, 58, 60) sts each sleeve.

Shape sleeve caps:
Dec row 3 (RS): *Work to B marker, sm, ssk, work to 2 sts before next B marker, k2tog, sm; rep from * once more, work to end. (4 sts dec'd.)
Rep Dec Row 3 on every RS row 3 (5, 7, 9, 13, 15) times more. 44 (42, 40, 38, 30, 28) sts rem each sleeve.
Dec row 4 (WS): *Work to B marker, sm, p2tog, work to 2 sts before next B marker, ssp, sm; rep from * once more, work to end. (4 sts dec'd.)
Rep Dec Rows 3-4 8 (7, 6, 5, 3, 2) times more. 10 (12, 14, 16, 16, 18) sts rem each sleeve.

Shape sleeve caps and front neck:
Right front:
Row 1 (RS): Work 8 sts and place them on a holder, work in patt to B marker, sm, ssk, turn. 18 (20, 21, 23, 24, 28) sts in right front.
Row 2 (WS): Sl1, work to end.
Row 3: K1, p2, k3tog, work to B marker, sm, ssk, turn.
Row 4: Rep Row 2.
Row 5: K1, p2, k2tog, work to B marker, sm, ssk, turn.
Row 6: Rep Row 2.
Rep Rows 5-6 1 (2, 3, 4, 4, 5) times more. Place these 15 (16, 16, 17, 18, 21) sts on a holder.

Left front:
Join yarn at front edge with WS facing.
Row 1 (WS): Work 8 sts and place them on a holder, work in patt to B marker, sm, p2tog, turn. 18 (20, 21, 23, 24, 28) sts in left front.
Row 2 (RS): Sl1, work to end.
Row 3: P1, k2, sssp, work to B marker, sm, p2tog, turn.
Row 4: Rep Row 2.
Row 5: P1, k2, ssp, work to B marker, sm, p2tog, turn.
Row 6: Rep Row 2.
Rep Rows 5-6 1 (2, 3, 4, 4, 5) times more. Place these 15 (16, 16, 17, 18, 21) sts on a holder.

Shape sleeve caps and back shoulders:
Join yarn with RS facing, 1 st before the right back B marker.
Row 1 (RS): Sl1, sm, work to next B marker, sm, ssk, turn.

Row 2 (WS): Sl1, sm, work to next B marker, sm, p2tog, turn.
Rep Rows 1-2 3 (4, 5, 6, 6, 7) times more. 54 (58, 60, 64, 66, 74) sts. Leave sts on needle with yarn attached.

FINISHING

With right sides facing, join right shoulder using a 3-needle bind off, BO next 24 (26, 28, 28, 30, 32) sts for back neck, join left shoulder using a 3-needle bind off.

Collar
With RS facing and smaller needle, work 8 sts from right front neck holder in patt, pick up and knit 1 st in every st and row around neck, work 8 sts from left front neck holder in patt. Count sts and adjust to a multiple of 4 on next rnd, if needed. Work in 2x2 Rib for 3½in / 9cm. BO in patt.

Graft underarms. Weave in ends and block, if desired, according to ball band instructions. Pin the zipper in place, starting from the hem and working up to 1¾in / 4cm past the beginning of the collar. Fold collar in half inward, covering the top end of the zipper but leaving its teeth exposed. Sew zipper and collar in place.

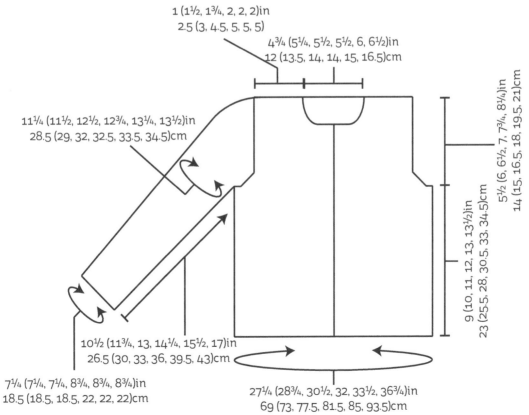

1 (1½, 1¾, 2, 2, 2)in
2.5 (3, 4.5, 5, 5, 5)

4¾ (5¼, 5½, 5½, 6, 6½)in
12 (13.5, 14, 14, 15, 16.5)cm

5½ (6, 6½, 7, 7¾, 8¾)in
14 (15, 16.5, 18, 19.5, 21)cm

11¼ (11½, 12½, 12¾, 13¼, 13½)in
28.5 (29, 32, 32.5, 33.5, 34.5)cm

9 (10, 11, 12, 13, 13½)in
23 (25.5, 28, 30.5, 33, 34.5)cm

10½ (11¾, 13, 14¼, 15½, 17)in
26.5 (30, 33, 36, 39.5, 43)cm

7¼ (7¼, 7¼, 8¾, 8¾, 8¾)in
18.5 (18.5, 18.5, 22, 22, 22)cm

27¼ (28¾, 30½, 32, 33½, 36¾)in
69 (73, 77.5, 81.5, 85, 93.5)cm

YARNS USED

The following yarns were used in this book. Many thanks to those companies who provided yarn support for this project.

Alba
thewoolshed.co.uk

Artesano
artesanoyarns.co.uk

Blue Sky Alpacas
blueskyalpacas.com

Cascade
cascadeyarns.com

Garnstudio DROPS
garnstudio.com

Jamieson & Smith
shetlandwoolbrokers.co.uk

KnitPicks
knitpicks.com

Lorna's Laces
lornaslaces.net

Malabrigo
malabrigoyarn.com

Rialto, Debbie Bliss
Kashmir, Louisa Harding
designeryarns.uk.com [UK] / knittingfever.com [US]

Rowan
knitrowan.com

ABBREVIATIONS

approx	approximately
beg	beginning
BO	bind off (cast off)
CC	contrast color
circ	circumference
cn	cable needle
CO	cast on
cont	continue / continuing
dec('d)	decrease / decreasing / decreased
dpn(s)	double pointed needle(s)
est	established
inc('d)	increase / increasing / increased
k	knit
k2tog	knit two stitches together
k3tog	knit three stitches together
kfb	knit into front and back of stitch
LH	left-hand
m1	make 1 stitch
m1L	make 1 left: insert left needle under horizontal strand between st just worked and next st from the front to the back, knit through the back loop
m1R	make 1 right: insert left needle under horizontal strand between st just worked and next st from the back to the front, knit through the front loop
MC	main color
p	purl
p2tog	purl two stitches together
patt(s)	pattern(s)
pfb	purl into front and back of stitch
pm	place marker
rem	remain(ing)
rep	repeat
rev St st	reverse stockinette stitch (stocking stitch)
RH	right-hand
RS	right side
rnd(s)	round(s)
sm	slip marker
ssk	slip 2 sts individually as if to knit, then knit those 2 stitches together through the back loops
sssk	slip 3 sts individually as if to knit, then knit those 3 stitches together through the back loops
ssp	slip 2 sts individually as if to knit, then purl those 2 stitches together through the back loops
sssp	slip 3 sts individually as if to knit, then purl those 3 stitches together through the back loops
sl	slip
st(s)	stitch(es)
St st	stockinette stitch (stocking stitch)
tbl	through the back loop
tog	together
w&t	wrap and turn (short rows)
WS	wrong side

ABOUT KATYA FRANKEL

© M. Waller

Katya Frankel is a knitwear designer and pattern writer. Her work regularly appears in numerous Interweave publications. She has also designed for Petite Purls and for the book More Knitting in the Sun for Kids. She lives in Newcastle upon Tyne, England.

ACKNOWLEDGMENTS

I would like to thank my family for their love and support. My husband, Daniel, and my kids, Sophie and Timothy, were so understanding and patient while I sat on the sofa with my laptop, wearing pajamas, rambling on about the gorgeous yarn trying to convince them I was working.

I am grateful to the Cooperative Press team for making this book a reality: Shannon Okey, the most energetic and positive person I have ever met, for her enthusiasm and encouragement, and for giving me the opportunity to put my vision onto paper; Elizabeth Green Musselman, the assistant editor, for editing my words and making me sound eloquent and clear; and Alexandra Virgiel, the tech editor, for making sure all the patterns are accurate and can be followed through, and that schematics have all the measurements that a knitter would ever need and fantastic charts.

Anthony, Joseph, Luke, Samuel, and Timothy, the handsome models, were such good sports and made the photo shoots a joy. They even tried to teach me a sliding tackle. (I must admit I was hopeless at it.) Chriss Coleman churned up perfect samples so quickly and gave sage knitting advice. Miriam Waller let us use her garden for all the last-minute photo sessions. Sophie Brettell provided the voice of reason and moral support when I needed it. And last but not least, thanks to Frankie Simmons for encouraging me to publish my designs in the first place.

Thank you all. - Katya

katyafrankel.com

ABOUT COOPERATIVE PRESS

partners in publishing

Cooperative Press (formerly anezka media) was founded in 2007 by Shannon Okey, a voracious reader as well as writer and editor, who had been doing freelance acquisitions work, introducing authors with projects she believed in to editors at various publishers.

Although working with traditional publishers can be very rewarding, there are some books that fly under their radar. They're too avant-garde, or the marketing department doesn't know how to sell them, or they don't think they'll sell 50,000 copies in a year.

5,000 or 50,000. Does the book matter to that 5,000? Then it should be published.

In 2009, Cooperative Press changed its named to reflect the relationships we have developed with authors working on books. We work together to put out the best quality books we can and share in the proceeds accordingly.

Thank you for supporting independent publishers and authors.

cooperativepress.com

CPSIA information can be obtained at www.ICGtesting.com
Printed in the USA
BVOW102343300113

312027BV00002B/3/P